VISIT VERSAILLES

Béatrix Saule

Director of the National Museum
of Versailles and Trianon

With the collaboration of

Mathieu da Vinha

Scientific director of the Château
de Versailles research centre

CHÂTEAU DE VERSAILLES

CONTENTS

MAP OF THE GROUND FLOOR OF THE CHÂTEAU

THE APARTMENTS OF THE PRINCES

THE APARTMENT OF THE DAUPHIN

1 The Guardroom
2 The First Antechamber
3 The Second Antechamber
4 The Bedchamber
5 The State Cabinet
6 The Library

THE APARTMENT OF THE DAUPHINE

7 The Private Cabinet
8 The Bedchamber
9 The State Cabinet
10 The Second Antechamber
11 The First Antechamber

MADAME VICTOIRE'S APARTMENT

12 The First Antechamber
13 The Second Antechamber or Peers' Room
14 The State Cabinet
15 The Bedchamber
16 The Private Cabinet
17 The Library

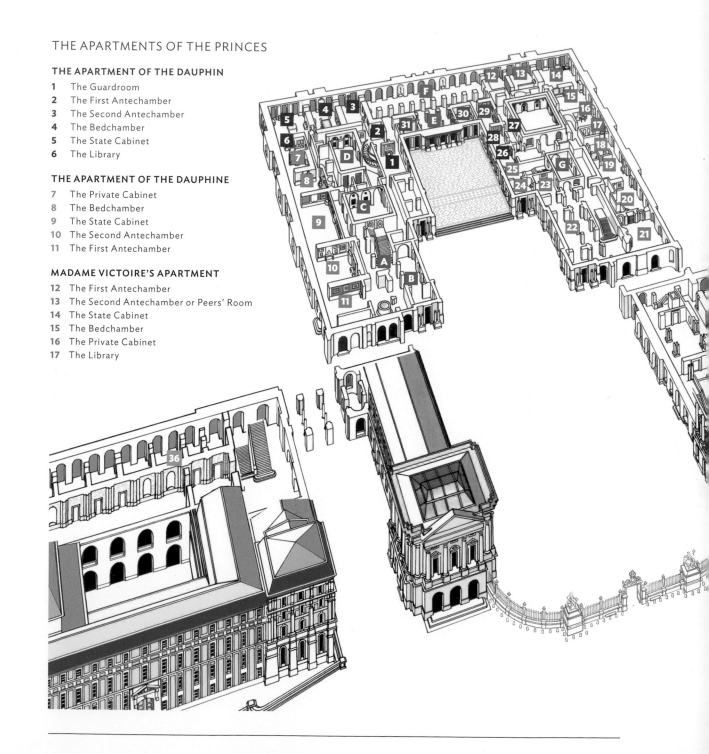

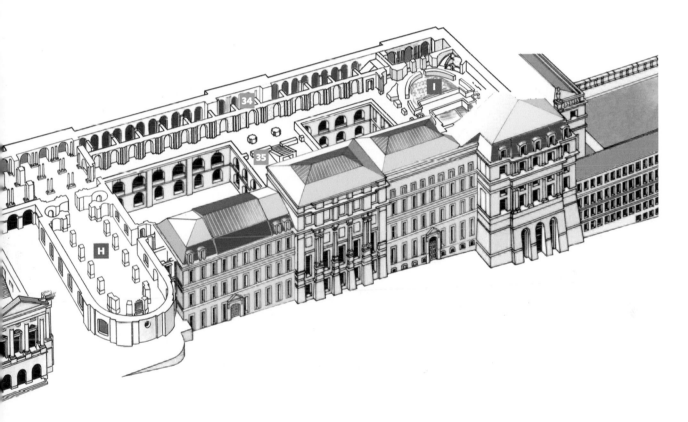

THE HISTORY OF FRANCE MUSEUM

MAP OF THE FIRST FLOOR OF THE CHÂTEAU

THE STATE APARTMENTS

THE KING'S GRAND APARTMENT

1 The Hercules Salon
2 The Abundance Salon
3 The Venus Salon
4 The Diana Salon
5 The Mars Salon
6 The Mercury Salon
7 The Apollo Salon

THE HALL OF MIRRORS AND ITS SALONS

8 The Salon of War
9 The Hall of Mirrors
10 The Salon of Peace

THE QUEEN'S SUITE

11 The Queen's Bedchamber
12 The Peers' Salon
13 The Antechamber for Grand Couvert repasts
14 The Queen's Guards Room

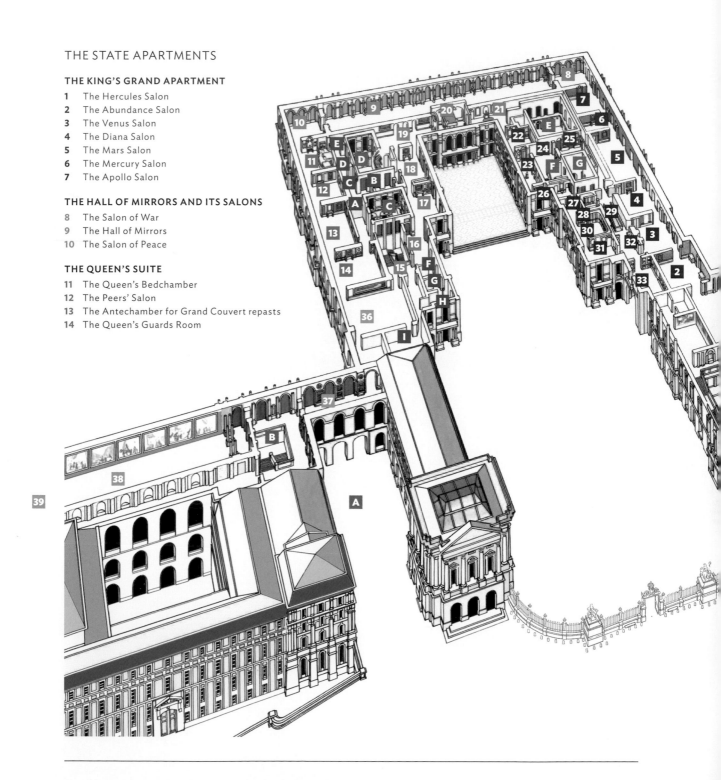

THE PRIVATE APARTMENTS

MARIE-ANTOINETTE'S PRIVATE APARTMENTS

A   The Library Annex
B   The Gilded Study
C   The Library
D   The Meridian Cabinet
E   The Duchess of Burgundy's Cabinet

MADAME DE MAINTENON'S APARTMENTS

F - G   The Antechambers
H   The Bedchamber
I   The State Cabinet

THE KING'S APARTMENTS

15   The Marble (or Queen's) Staircase
16   The loggia also giving access
     to the King's apartment
17   The King's Guards Room
18   The First Antechamber
     or antechamber for Grand Couvert repasts
19   The Second Antechamber
     or Œil-de-Bœuf Antechamber
20   The King's Bedchamber
21   The Council Cabinet

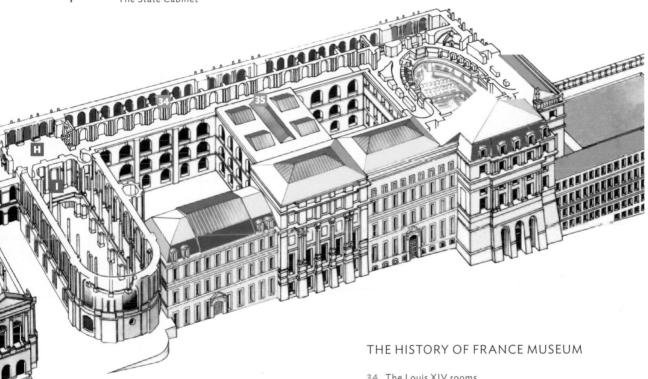

THE HISTORY OF FRANCE MUSEUM

34   The Louis XIV rooms
35   The 19th century rooms
36   The Coronation Room
37   The Merchants' Room or 1792 Room
38   The Battle Gallery
39   The 1830 Room

A   The Princes' Courtyard
B   The Princes' Staircase
C   The Queen's Courtyard
D   The Dauphin's Courtyard
E   The Stags' Courtyard
F   The King's Staircase
G   The King's Private Staircase
H   The Chapel Salon
I   The Royal Tribune of the Chapel

THE KING'S PRIVATE APARTMENTS

22   Louis XV and Louis XVI's Bedchamber
23   The Clock Cabinet
24   The Dogs' Antechamber
25   The Post-Hunt Dining Room
26   The Inner Cabinet or Corner Cabinet
27   The Dispatch Cabinet
28   The Golden Dishes Room
29   The Bathroom
30   Louis XVI's Library
31   The Porcelain Dining Room
32   The Buffet Room
33   Louis XVI's Games Room

VERSAILLES, SEAT OF THE OLD MONARCHY

When the six-year-old dauphin Louis was introduced to hunting in 1607, his father Henri chose the woods around Versailles. The cherished memories of these times inspired Louis XIII to build an initial hunting lodge in 1623-1624. But the building was immediately ridiculed. The king then commissioned his architect Philibert Le Roy to undertake reconstruction which, although bigger and with the proportions of a vast lordly residence, was still far from royal. Despite several modifications by the architect, "the little house of cards", as Saint-Simon dubbed it, remained unchanged until the sovereign's death in 1643. It was also somewhat by chance that the future Louis XIV discovered Versailles for the first time in 1641 since his father sent him there with his brother Philippe to escape a smallpox epidemic in Saint-Germain. He was to return ten years later to enjoy the pleasures of the hunt. He would henceforth return regularly for his personal amusement.

Although Louis XIII had a hunting lodge built with its own gardens on the site, it was Louis XIV who truly created Versailles. Removed from the rebellious people of Paris, yet within reach of the city, the site offered plenty of opportunity to build: it thus fulfilled the king's desire to gather his Court around him, something that no other royal residence in the area could offer. It was he who gave the palace its grandeur; it was he who mapped out its destiny. Between 1682 and 1789, with a slight hiatus between 1715 and 1722, Versailles was the seat of

◑ (PREVIOUS DOUBLE PAGE) Pierre Denis Martin, *View of the Château de Versailles from the Place d'Armes, 1722.* Oil on canvas, 139 × 150 cm.
◐ Israël Silvestre, *View of the Château de Versailles garden side circa 1650,* 17th century. Etching, 9 × 17.3 cm.

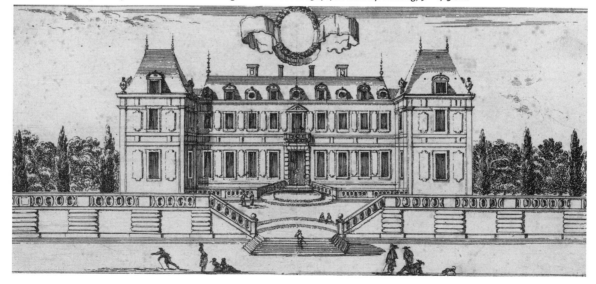

⊙ Adam Frans Van der Meulen, *Arrival of Louis XIV preceded by bodyguards with view over the old Château de Versailles in 1669, circa 1669*. Oil on canvas, diameter: 56 cm.

the absolute monarchy and became its symbol, since the place itself, modelled according to the Sun King's wishes, reflects the way he conceived power.

The dwelling place of all power

In an absolute monarchy, all power comes from the King. In Versailles, Louis XIV was Master of his own house, just as he was Master of the kingdom that he governed through intermediaries that owed him

everything. Excluded from affairs of government, the Nobility no longer held any real power, yet they nonetheless felt the need to appear at Court. It was there that the King dispensed favours: offices, land, titles, pensions, etc. In this society founded on prestige and appearances, emulation was constant, luxury compulsory, life extravagant. In this way, Louis XIV "had a hold" over his courtiers. It was he who had to dominate in every way; in his eyes, the exercise and

⬆ Pierre Patel, the father, *View of the Château and gardens of Versailles, from the Avenue de Paris in 1668*, 1668. Oil on canvas, 115 × 161 cm.

outward signs of power were one and the same thing. His residence had to be the biggest and the most beautiful and its décor loaded with symbols to his glory. The number of servants, in the noble sense of the term, assembled in the King's House had to be the greatest and his Court had to be attended by the most people; between 3000 and 10,000 courtiers, depending on the day. At the end of the reign, the château itself could host 4,000 residents, while outbuildings in the town housed 2,700. This huge crowd had to be strictly regulated. Etiquette and its constraints – who had access to the King, who had the right to sit down in his presence, who was ranked above whom, etc. – may seem pointless to us today. However, etiquette was essential, since it served to confirm ranks, the primacy of the King, in short the hierarchy within the Court. It applied to the Sovereign's most private moments – getting up in the morning, going to bed at night, mealtimes, going for walks – which were perceived as acts of State when acts of State appeared to be the King's personal acts. Another specific feature of Versailles, and something which naturally astonished foreigners, was that both the gardens and the inside of the Château were largely open to the public. Anyone, be they a member of the Court or otherwise, could see the King when he crossed his State Apartments to go to the Chapel. They could even go right into his Bedchamber, as long as he was not there. All these functions – representation, government, accommodation and service – explain the lay-out of the place. But it was not built in a day.

Fifty years of building work

When Louis XIV came to have fun in his father's hunting lodge at the start of his own reign in 1661 and ordered the first alterations, even he could never have imagined that this small building, consisting at the

↻ Eugène Lami, The supper given by Napoleon III in the Opera House of the Château of Versailles, *visit by Queen Victoria to Paris in 1855*, 1855. Watercolour, 48.5 × 66.5 cm.

time of the structures that surround the future Marble Courtyard, was to become the core of a vast complex. During this youthful period, he initiated building work inside – entrusted to Charles Le Brun – and outside, initially favouring the extension of the grounds and the gardens, immediately entrusted to André Le Nôtre, which became the setting for festivities so extraordinary that Versailles became known throughout Europe. It was the day after the Great royal entertainment of 1668 that the king noted the smallness of the structure and so decided on the first extensions. Le Vau and d'Orbay, the king's architects, enveloped the old château with three main buildings overlooking the grounds. The new buildings constructed in stone and according to the tastes of the time – a baroque Roman villa style – contrasted so starkly with the brick, stone and slate architecture dating from the time of Louis XIII, that there appeared to be two châteaus,

slotted one into the other. Le Brun, Chief Painter to the King, provided the drawings for all the internal décor of the State Apartments and for the sculptures of the fountains with their multiple water effects in the parterres, avenues and groves. Apollo, the Sun God with whom the King was identified, reigned throughout. Between the King's apartment, which extends to the north, and that of the Queen, to the south, the central facade on the garden hosts an Italian-style terrace with a central fountain. Louis XIV took pleasure in seeing his palace rise up and would play at architect, adding notes to the drawings, correcting a perspective or alignment and, when Colbert, the superintendent general of buildings, asked how much detail his work reports should contain, the King replied "details of everything".

But this new château no longer sufficed and the arrival on the scene of Jules Hardouin-Mansart greatly

modified the physiognomy of the château allowing it to assume the dimensions we know today.

In 1677, this accelerated building work reflected the determination of Louis XIV to move the Court and Government to Versailles permanently. Thus began an immense building project, which, in spite of the tens of thousands of men working on it, was far from complete on 6 May 1682 when the king actually moved in to the "palace still filled with workmen" according to the Provost Marshal. Under the direction of J. Hardouin-Mansart the built-on area was increased five-fold, with the construction of two stables (1679-1682), Ministers' Wings (1679-1682), the Grand Lodgings (1682-1684), the South (1679-1682) and North (1685-1689) wings and the Grand Trianon (1687-1688). As of 1678, the Hall of Mirrors replaced the central terrace on the first floor.

The interiors were constantly renovated, the groves continuously redesigned, the water pipe work increasingly ambitious. But wars towards the end of the king's reign hampered the progress of the projects. The fifth and last chapel was only officially opened in 1710, albeit unfinished. It was the king's determination and fifty years of hard work, hesitations, trials and tribulations that ultimately led to the creation of a whole where everything was carefully mastered – both nature and men – where everything was ordered and structured around a line passing through the centre of the royal residence, where the king's bedchamber had been located since 1701.

Outwardly nothing changed

On the death of Louis XIV in 1715, the court left Versailles for Vincennes and then Paris. It was Louis XV

⊙ Victor Bachereau-Reverchon,
Episode from the war of 1870,
19th century. Oil on canvas,
77 × 100 cm.

⊙ William Orpen, *Signing of
the peace treaty by the German
delegation in the Hall of Mirrors on
28 June 1919*, 1921. Oil on canvas,
152.4 × 127 cm. London, Imperial
War Museum Collections.

who, in June 1722 aged twelve, asked to return to the residence of his great grandfather. The château had suffered for seven years and the governor, largely thanks to the fountain displays every second Sunday, managed to maintain a semblance of normal activity. This hiatus did not lead to the end of this court "machinery", which had become an attribute of royalty and Versailles in its own right. Up until 1789, it was imposed on Louis XV then on Louis XVI, no doubt both imprisoned by this burdensome heritage, who were required to reproduce the same customs in the same places as their forefather. Despite being increasingly seen as restrictive, expensive and antiquated, no reforms could be made without affecting too many privileges. Versailles continued to function in the same way as it had under the Great Monarch, outwardly at least. Unlike Louis XVI

who was not a building king, Louis XV perfected the work of his great-grandfather, with this same spirit of magnificence, commissioning the decoration of the Hercules Salon, the Neptune Basin and the Opera.

But in addition to this ceremonial life, these sovereigns also led a simple personal existence, sparing them from the constraints of etiquette. The fashion was for elegance and privacy. Nooks within the château, small apartments and private cabinets multiplied, housing a very small circle of family and friends, in décors constantly updated to reflect the tastes of their time. The greatest sophistication was reflected in the décor, the conversation, the music, the food, etc.

Kings and Queens too frequently withdrew to their own private apartments or to Trianon. Louis XV, and especially Louis XVI and Marie-Antoinette, adopted this attitude with no heed for the consequences. The sovereigns neglected the very principle of the French monarchy: its accessibility, or at the very least, its visibility. Moreover, the simplification of practices, with Louis XVI preferring to dress himself, led to a deconsecration of royal persons. This was reinforced by the reforms to the King's Household introduced as of 1780. The elimination of hundreds of servant posts, which nonetheless enabled considerable savings, was poorly received by the court which was openly critical of these changes. The courtiers grew tired of it all, wondering "What's the point of coming to Versailles?" On the eve of the Revolution, the Court was often deserted; the nobility had distanced itself from the King.

From the Revolution to the present day

The Revolution emptied the château of its furnishings but spared the building itself. All of the paintings left for the Louvre Museum and the furniture was sold, with only a few exceptions. The new regime understood the historical and symbolic importance of the site. There was talk of using it for the people's education but, after several proposals, the projects were abandoned, one after the other. After years of neglect, it was restored first by Napoleon I, and then by Kings Louis XVIII and Charles X, both brothers of Louis XVI. But none dared make it the seat of power: moving into Versailles would constitute provocation; it would be too suggestive of a return to the Ancien Régime and its privileges. For a while, nobody knew what to do with it and demolition was even considered, but the château was ultimately saved by King Louis-Philippe. In a spirit of national reconciliation, in 1833, the "King of the French" decided to turn it into a museum, dedicated to "all of France's glories". Opened in 1837, the History Galleries recount a concise story of France's history in monumental form, from the foundation of the kingdom to modern times.

Several themed rooms – Africa, the Crimea, etc. – were envisaged but not all had been completed by the end of the July monarchy in 1848. There then followed a period of transition for the palace and Napoleon III, as under the Ancien Régime, used it for numerous parties and receptions during the Second Empire. The advent of the 3rd Republic, after the defeat at Sudan against Prussia, was chaotic and as of 1870 Versailles served as a refuge for the future governmental system. In March 1871, the Opera Royal was fitted out in less than ten days by the architect of the estate and the assembly in order to host ministers, committees and all elected representatives. Parliament sat there until December 1876 when the Congress Room was completed in the south wing, able to accommodate all senators and deputies. It was they who would elect the President of the Republic at Versailles until 1953, from Matrice de Mac Mahon through to René Coty.

Alongside the History Museum, since the start of the 20th century, curators and architects have focused on restoring and refurnishing the royal and princely apartments that make up the core of the château, at the same time adding to the collections of paintings and sculptures that still occupy its wings.

The palace crossed eras and endured the threats of wars with works placed in storage, fully demonstrating its central role in the history of France. In fact, during World War One, the Hall of Mirrors accommodated wounded soldiers while the peace treaty ending hostilities was signed there on 28 June 1919. The showcase for French know-how during the Enlightenment, history museum, national palace and symbol of the Republic, Versailles was also the theatre for numerous international events: the receptions of Queen Elizabeth II in 1957 and the US president John Fitzgerald Kennedy in 1961, the summit of heads of states and governments of the leading industrialised nations (G7) in 1982, etc.

More than three and a half centuries after its creation, the estate, despite having lost its hunting grounds, still remains vast, with its three châteaux, its garden, its park and outbuildings: 830 hectares of grounds, 20 km of roads, the same amount of closing walls, 350,000 trees and as many flowers planted every year, 35 km of water pipes, 13 hectares of roofs, 2,143 windows, 67 staircases...

The sheer scale and order of the Sun King's château inspired other European sovereigns. Although its most famous replica is that of Louis II of Bavaria in Herrenchiemsee, many monarchs have coveted Versailles of their own such as Csar Peter I in Saint Petersburg or Peterhof, the king of Spain in Madrid or La Granja, the Empress Maria-Theresa in Schönbrunn, the Margrave Charles-Guillaume at the château of Karlsruhe or the Bourbons of Naples in Caserta.

The exhibition of the chateau's history and the Louis XIV rooms.

In the North Wing, between the Chapel and the Opera, the eleven ground-floor rooms feature a gallery on the château's history. After a general introduction to the château and its estate, the visitor discovers the main stages of construction since the first Versailles of Louis XIII, the palace of the Sun King, the gardens, changes in the 18th and 19th centuries, through to the Versailles of today. Multimedia rooms facilitate understanding of this transformation of Versailles via its different facets: the hunting lodge, the royal residence, the history museum and the national palace. On the first floor, acting as a counterpoint to the ground-floor gallery, can be found the palace's extensive collections relating to the Grand Siècle – paintings, sculptures and furniture. The guardian figure of Louis XIV serves as a guide line for the visit. The first four rooms offer a biographical presentation of the childhood of the so–vereign and the regency of Anne of Austria; the royal family; the assumption of power and the politics of the kingdom; and the court at Versailles. For the last six rooms, a themed presentation is preferred, based around major figures of the "king of war", the "very Christian king", the "artists of Louis XIV" as well as the principal royal residences and their décors.

⊙ View of the Louis XIV rooms.

◔ View of the exhibition of the Chateau's history.

VERSAILLES, PALAIS ROYAL

THE STATE APARTMENTS
THE PRIVATE APARTMENTS
THE APARTMENTS OF THE PRINCES

In front of the entry gate, a wide open space separates the stables from the château: this is the Place d'Armes, where the king inspected his army's regiments. Beyond the gate lie three courtyards, one after the other: the Cour d'Honneur, flanked by the Ministers' wings, followed by the Royal Courtyard closed off by a second gate, and finally the Marble Courtyard. It was through this second gate that access was gained to the actual "royal dwelling" and only the most esteemed personalities were permitted to pass through in their carriages. The Royal Courtyard then entered is overlooked by buildings which differ from the others in terms of scale and the material used to construct them: stone. Work began on these buildings at the end of the reign of Louis XV. They were designed by the architect Gabriel who had the façades on the town side completely rebuilt in a classical style that was considered more noble at the time. The architecture of the façades, in brick and stone, topped by high slate roofs, actually dates back to the era of the first Château de Versailles built for Louis XIII, as Louis XIV retained it and had it extended in the same style. Although reworked, this original building still forms the heart of the château today.

◐ View of the Marble Courtyard, the Château and the Grande Perspective.

THE KING'S GRAND APARTMENT

The Grand Apartment now consists of seven salons or drawing rooms overlooking the gardens on the north side through tall, floor-to-ceiling-height windows, a novelty at the time of its creation in the 1670s. This prestigious sequence of rooms, which was laid out in the usual style of princely apartments – antechambers, guardrooms, antechamber, bedchamber, state cabinet - was designed to serve as a ceremonial apartment, in other words, as a backdrop for the official acts of the sovereign. It is for this reason that they were decorated with such sumptuousness and in the style of the Italian palaces of the era. The Premier Peintre (or Chief Painter to the King) Charles Le Brun, who was also the director of the Royal Academy of Painting and Sculpture and director of the Crown furniture manufactory, provided all the designs for the ceilings, the precious marble panelling, the furniture… right down to the door locks. But Louis XIV soon got into the habit of carrying out the core of his "royal duty" in his private apartment overlooking the Marble courtyard. So this Grand Apartment became a thoroughfare and a place for people to be received. During the day, it was open to everyone – French as well as foreign – who came to see the king there when he passed through on his way to the chapel or to admire the most splendid paintings in the royal collections. But three evenings per week, between All Saints Day and Easter, it was reserved for courtiers. From 7 o'clock to 10 o'clock, "soirées d'appartement" or court receptions were held consisting of light meals, music, dancing and games.

⬆ Jean Garnier, *Allegory of Louis XIV, protector of the Arts and Sciences* (detail), 18th century. Oil on canvas, 163 × 204 cm.
➡ View of the series of rooms in the King's Grand Apartment.

THE HERCULES SALON

The State Apartment's first salon, the Hercules Salon, was actually the last one to be created, at the end of the reign of Louis XIV. The location had previously been occupied by the château's chapel, created in 1682 on two floors and used until 1710, when it was replaced by the current chapel. To decorate this new salon, the monumental painting by Veronese, *Christ at Supper with Simon*, painted for the refectory of the Servite convent in Venice around 1570, was placed there in 1712. In 1664, the Doge had given the painting to Louis XIV to thank the latter for supporting him against the Turks. Interrupted for a period of ten years following the death of the Sun King, work on the Hercules Salon lasted until 1736, when François Lemoine completed the ceiling painting showing *The Apotheosis of Hercules*, designed to depict the fact that "Virtue elevates man above himself". Through its effect, this vast allegorical composition containing 142 figures was intended to rival the great masterpieces of the Italian fresco painters but it was actually done on canvases that were then mounted on the ceiling, i.e. that were stuck onto the medium. The process was so exhausting that, in spite of the success his work met with, the young painter committed suicide shortly afterwards.

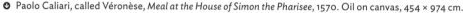

⊙ Paolo Caliari, called Véronèse, *Meal at the House of Simon the Pharisee*, 1570. Oil on canvas, 454 × 974 cm.

THE ABUNDANCE SALON

During "soirées d'appartement", the Abundance Salon was where refreshments were taken; coffee, wines and liqueurs were available on a sideboard. It was also the antechamber of Louis XIV's Cabinet of Curiosities or Rarities (now occupied by Louis XVI's Games room) which could be reached through the door at the end. The king liked to show his distinguished guests the silver vases, gemstones and medals that were kept there and which inspired the décor of the arch. In particular, the large royal ship represented above the door can be admired. The king's ship, a precious object in the form of a dismasted boat, was placed on the sovereign's table for grand occasions or, of course, on the sideboard. A symbol of power to be saluted by every passer-by, it contained the sovereign's napkin.

THE VENUS SALON

Along with the Diana Salon, this salon represented the main access to the State Apartments since the state staircase, known as the "Ambassadors' Staircase" (destroyed in 1752) led to this room. They were also referred to as the two marble antechambers. On state evenings, tables were set out with baskets of flowers, pyramids of fresh and rare fruit, such as oranges and lemons as well as crystallized fruit and marzipan. As is the case with each of the subsequent rooms, this salon is named after a planet, a theme linked to the solar myth that inspired all the décors at Versailles in the 1670s. Here the planet Venus is represented on the ceiling, in the form of the goddess of Love, who was linked with this planet in Ancient Greece. The other paintings, adorning the spring of the vault (ceiling panels), were designed to depict the actions of ancient heroes relating both to the planet of the same name and the actions of Louis XIV: hence the panel representing Augustus presiding over circus games should be seen as referring to the famous carousel of 1662 given in honour of the queen and the one depicting Alexander marrying Roxane as evoking the wedding of Louis XIV. Of all the rooms in the sequence, the Venus Salon has the most baroque décor. It is the only room where Le Brun created a dialogue between the architectures, the sculptures and the paintings, sometimes real and sometimes false: the marble pilasters and columns are echoed in the perspectives painted by Jacques Rousseau, and two trompe l'œil statues on the window side are a repost to the figure of Louis XIV by Jean Warin.

THE DIANA SALON

Like the Venus Salon, the Diana Salon served as a vestibule to the State Apartments and, during the time of Louis XIV, as a billiard room during "soirées d'appartement". Two special platforms were reserved for the ladies who applauded whenever the king, who was very skilled at the game, hit a good shot. So much so that the room was also called "the room of applause". In Greek Antiquity, Diana the Goddess of Hunting was associated with the moon, for her coldness. She was also the sister of Apollo, the Sun God. The ceiling panels are adorned with hunting scenes involving heroes from Antiquity. Here, the allusion is transparent as it is well known that Louis XIV was a great huntsman.

The central part of the ceiling painted by Gabriel Blanchard depicts *Diana presiding over navigation and hunting*. On the fireplace, the painting by Charles de La Fosse depicts *The Sacrifice of Iphigenia* and, opposite, above the console, the one by Gabriel Blanchard *Diana and Endymion*. The classical busts come from the collections of Cardinal de Mazarin bequeathed to Louis XIV.

⬆ Gian Lorenzo Bernini, known as Le Bernin, *Bust of Louis XIV*, 1665. White marble, 105 × 95.5 × 46.5 cm.

THE MARS SALON

As well as being a planet, Mars is also the God of War. The choice of this military theme that was to inspire the decoration throughout this large room can be explained by the fact that it was originally designed as the guard-room for the ceremonial apartment. It was subsequently used for music and dancing on state evenings and hence came to be commonly known as the "ballroom". Court dances were very formal and required numerous rehearsals; princes took part in them, sometimes alongside professional dancers. On either side of the fireplace, two platforms, installed in 1684 then removed in 1750, were intended for the musicians.

In the centre of the ceiling, Claude Audran painted *Mars on a chariot drawn by wolves*. The work is flanked by two compositions: one, on the east side, by Jouvenet: *Victory supported by Hercules followed by Abundance and Felicity*; the other, on the west side, by Houasse: *Terror, Fury and Fear taking possession of earthly powers*. Four paintings by Simon Vouet, originally in the Château de Saint-Germain-en-Laye, are placed above the doors: *Temperance*, *Prudence*, *Justice* and *Fortitude*. While *David playing the harp* by Dominichino, Louis XIV's favourite painting placed above the fireplace, used to be in the alcove of the King's bedchamber in Louis XIV's time and was a matching piece to a *Saint Jean in Patmos*, by Innocenzo da Imola, at the time attributed to Raphael.

To the left of the fireplace can be seen *The Family of Darius before Alexander*, by Charles Le Brun and on the right *The Pilgrims of Emmaus*, based on the Veronese painting (previously the original): placed together as matching pieces, they reflect a determination to show that French painters could now rival the very best Italian masters. On the side walls are two ceremonial portraits: *Louis XV* and *Maria Leszczinska*, both painted by Carle Van Loo.

THE MERCURY SALON

Originally, the Mercury Salon was the ceremonial bed-chamber of the State Apartment, hence the name "bed-chamber", although the bed in question was taken away during the winter to make room for games tables. Until 1689, when Louis XIV was forced to melt them down in order to finance the war of the League of Augsburg, tables, mirrors, firedogs and chandeliers of solid silver, magnificently chiselled by the silversmiths of the Les Gobelins manufactory, adorned the floors, walls, ceilings and fireplace. A balustrade, also made of silver, separated the alcove from the rest of the room. Brocades – fabrics woven using gold and silver threads – hung on the walls and the bed but these too were sent to the Mint, this time to support the Spanish War of Succession. One of the rare occasions on which the Mercury Salon was used as a bedchamber was for the proclamation of the Duke of Anjou, the grandson of Louis XIV, as King of Spain: the young prince slept in

it for three weeks, before departing for his new country. It is also in this room that the body of Louis XIV was displayed from 2 to 10 September 1715.

The ceiling painted by Jean-Baptiste de Champaigne depicts *Mercury on his chariot drawn by two cockerels*. The vaulted ceiling panels are decorated with four paintings: on the left, on the Mars Salon side, *Augustus receiving an Ambassador of the Indians*; at the end, opposite the windows, *Ptolemy consulting scholars in his library*; on the right, on the window side, *Alexander and Aristotle* receiving from this prince a variety of strange animals for which he writes their story. The bed that can be seen now is the one Louis-Philippe had installed in the King's Bedchamber when he converted Versailles into a museum. Only the celebrated automation clock that its designer, Antoine Morand, gave to Louis XIV in 1706 has been returned to the place it occupied up until the Revolution.

Games at Versailles

"SOIRÉES D'APPARTEMENT"

As of 1676, Madame de Sévigné wrote of the astounding entertainment at the Château de Versailles but, the arrival of the royal family in 1682, with the virtual completion of the King's State Apartment, institutionalised these "soirées d'appartement", giving them an unmatched prestige. These were receptions hosted by the king, from All Saints Day to Easter, generally three times a week to a limited court. They represented a special moment of communion between the sovereign and his subjects since normal etiquette was put on hold for the evening as revealed by the *Mercure Galant* gazette: "we enjoyed total freedom to speak and everyone would discuss according to the pleasure of the conversation. (...) The King, the Queen and the entire Royal Household descended from their grandeur to take part in entertainments with members of the National Assembly who had never before known such an honour". These "soirées" were held between the gallery and the Abundance Salon. Each room had a specific purpose. In December 1682, the Apollo Salon was devoted to dance, the Diana Salon to the games of the king, queen and royal family, while the Mars Salon accommodated other players. The Mercury Salon was reserved for billiards. Further on, the Venus Salon hosted light meals consisting in fruit such as oranges and lemons, candied items and a wide variety of dried jam. Finally, the Abundance Salon hosted sideboards: one for hot drinks - coffee and chocolate - and the other two for liqueurs, sorbets, different types of fruit cordials and wine.

🔽 Antoine Trouvain, *First apartment, the Portico game* (detail), 1694. Print, 34 × 44.5 cm.

THE APOLLO SALON

The Apollo Salon, dedicated to the Sun God, God of the Arts and Peace with whom Louis XIV identified himself, was the most sumptuous of all. This can still be seen today in the décor of the ceiling where all the paintings – central composition, panels and corner pieces – are in glorious colour and the sculptures are in the round and all gilded. But everything else has gone: the silver furniture, and in particular the 2.6-metre-high throne, was melted down in 1689. A gilded wooden chair, the style of which evolved with the various reigns, replaced the throne of Louis XIV. It was placed on a platform covered with a Persian carpet with a gold background and under a canopy. The hangings which, as in all royal households, were changed according to the season, were in crimson velvet punctuated by eighteen strips of gold and silver embroidery in the winter, and silver and gold embroideries on a silk background in the summer. On the ceiling, *Apollo on his chariot drawn by four horses and accompanied by the seasons* was painted by Charles de La Fosse. The portrait of Louis XIV by Hyacinthe Rigaud is a matching piece for the portrait of Louis XVI by Antoine-François Callet.

◐ General view of the Apollo ceiling with, in the centre, the painting by Charles de La Fosse, *Apollo on his chariot drawn by four horses and accompanied by the seasons*, 1672-1681. Marouflaged canvas, diameter: 490 cm.
◑ Hyacinthe Rigaud, *Full-length portrait of Louis XIV aged 63 in royal dress*, 1702. Oil on canvas, 313 × 205 cm.

THE HALL OF MIRRORS AND ITS SALONS

Following the victory over the three powers united against France – Germany, Spain and Holland – represented in the Salon of War, the 73-metre-long hall exalts France's political, economic and artistic success. Political success: the twenty-seven compositions on the vaulted ceiling painted by Le Brun illustrate the glorious history of Louis XIV during the first eighteen years of his personal government, from 1661 until the Nijmegen Peace Treaty. Thus, military and diplomatic victories, along with reforms to reorganise the kingdom, are illustrated in the form of classical allegories. Economic prosperity: through their dimensions and number, the 357 mirrors adorning the seventeen arcades opposite the windows testify to the fact that the emerging French mirror industry was capable of challenging Venice's monopoly on mirrors, considered to be objects of immense luxury at the time. Artistic success: the Rance marble pilasters are adorned with a new design - the so-called "French order" - of gilded bronze capitals; created by Le Brun at the request of Colbert, it depicts the emblems of France: a fleur de lys surmounted by the royal sun between two French cockerels.

⬆ Claude Hallé, *The Doge of Genoa offering his apologies to Louis XIV* (detail), *circa* 1710. Oil on canvas, 343 × 603 cm.

THE SALON OF WAR

Mansart began building work on the Salon of War in 1678. The decoration, completed by Le Brun in 1686, exalted the military conquests of the Dutch War (1672-1678), ending in the Treaty of Nijmegen. The walls are covered with marble panels decorated with six trophies and chutes d'armes in gilded bronze. The wall on the Apollo Salon side features an oval low relief in stucco depicting *Louis XIV on horseback trampling upon his enemies*. This masterpiece by Coysevox is surmounted by two gilded Renommés and supported by two prisoners in chains. Below, in the bas-relief covering the opening to a false fireplace, *Clio is writing the history of the King for the future*. The ceiling, which was painted by Le Brun, shows in the centre *Armed France seated on a cloud, surrounded by Victories*. A portrait of Louis XIV adorns her shield. The three vanquished enemies are displayed in the vaulted ceiling panels: Germany, kneeling, with an eagle, a threatening Spain with a roaring lion and Holland, upside down on a lion; the fourth represents Bellone, goddess of war, in a rage between Rebellion and Discord.

⊙ Military trophies decorating the Salon of War.

THE HALL OF MIRRORS

The Grande Galerie or Great Gallery as it was named in the 17th century, was a thoroughfare and meeting place frequented daily by courtiers and the visiting public. It was only rarely used for ceremonial purposes, when the sovereigns wanted to lend as much glamour as possible to diplomatic receptions or the entertainment (balls and games) provided for the weddings of princes. For the former, the throne was set up on a platform at the end of the hall, at the Salon of Peace end, the arcade to which was closed off. Only rarely did the display of power achieve such a degree of ostentation; hence the Doge of Genoa in 1685 and the ambassadors of Siam (1686), Persia (1715) and the Ottoman Empire (1742) had to cross the entire length of the hall, under the eyes of the Court assembled on either side on terraces! There were also the wedding festivities of the Duke of Burgundy, the grandson of Louis XIV in 1697, the son of Louis XV in 1745, with the Infanta of Spain then in 1747 with Maria-Josepha of Saxony and finally the masked ball for the marriage of Marie-Antoinette and the Dauphin, the future Louis XVI, in May 1770... It is also here that on 28 June 1919, the Treaty of Versailles bringing an end to the First World War was signed. Since then, the Presidents of the Republic have continued to play host to the official guests of France in this hall.

THE SALON OF PEACE

The Salon of Peace presents the same décor of marble panels and gilded and chiselled bronze trophies of arms as the Salon of War, which is symmetrical to it. However, Le Brun adorned the dome and the ceiling panels with the benefits of peace given by France to Europe. From the end of the reign of Louis XIV, this salon was separated from the hall by a mobile partition and considered to be part of the Queen's Suite, forming, as it then did, its last room. It was here that, under the reign of Louis XV, Maria Leszczinska gave secular or religious music concerts every Sunday which were to play an important role in the musical life of Versailles. It was also here that Marie-Antoinette hosted her card games during the next reign.

The ceiling, which is the work of Le Brun, depicts *Victorious France offering an olive branch to the Powers that had united against her*. The vaulted ceiling panels depict *Spain, Christian Europe at peace, Germany and Holland*. Above the fireplace, the large oval canvas painted by François Lemoine in 1729 shows *Louis XV giving peace to Europe*. The gilded bronze "firedogs" in the form of lions, created on the basis of a model by Boizot, were put there at the time of Marie-Antoinette.

◐ Charles Nicolas Cochin the Younger, *Masked ball given for the marriage of Louis Dauphin of France to Maria Theresa of Spain* (detail), 18th century. Watercolour, brown ink, lead pencil, quill, white highlights, 44.3 × 76.4 cm. Paris, the Louvre museum, graphic arts department.

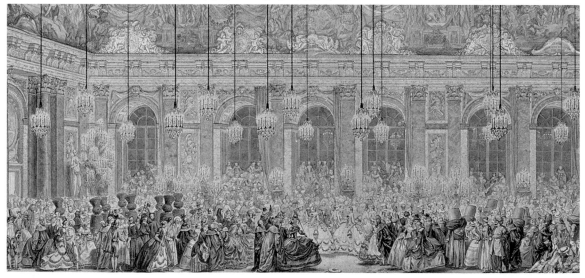

THE QUEEN'S SUITE

Overlooking the South Parterre, the Queen's Suite is symmetrical to the King's Grand Apartment. After the decision by Louis XV to take over the Queen's private apartment on the marble courtyard following the death of Queen Maria Theresa in 1683, it was occupied successively by two dauphines, Marie-Christine of Bavaria and Marie-Adelaide of Savoy, then by the two queens, Maria Leszczinska (from 1725 to 1768) and Marie-Antoinette (from 1770, when she was still dauphine, until 1789) But, unlike the sovereign who, from the reign of Louis XIV, abandoned his State Apartments, the queen continued to occupy hers, which explains why the décor was altered several times during the course of the 18th century. It comprises four rooms which can be toured today, from the bedchamber to the guardroom, the exact opposite to the way it was used under the Ancien Régime.

↑ Jean-Baptiste-André Gautier d'Agoty, *Marie-Antoinette playing the harp in her bedchamber at Versailles* (detail), 18th century. Gouache, 67.5 × 54.5 cm.
➋ View of the fireplace in the Queen's bedchamber with the bust of *Marie-Antoinette, Queen of France*, by Félix Lecomte, 1783. Marble, 86 × 50 × 28 cm.

✿ François Boucher, *Allegory of Charity*, 1735. Marouflaged grisaille painting in a rocaille cornice frame in the centre of the west arch.

THE QUEEN'S BEDCHAMBER

The bedchamber is the suite's principal room, where the queen would most often be found. She slept there, often joined by the king. In the mornings, she received both during and after her toilette, a time in the court timetable that was as regulated as when the king rose from his bed. It was also here that royal births took place in public: nineteen "Children of France" were born there. The décor preserves the memory of the three queens who occupied the room: the partitioning of the ceiling dates back to Queen Maria Theresa, but the paintings in grisaille by Boucher were done for Maria Leszczinska, as was the panelling. All these features have been preserved since the time of Marie-Antoinette, for whom only the furniture and fireplace were delivered new.

When the château was invaded by the mob on 6 October 1789, Marie-Antoinette managed to escape through one of the two small alcove doors which give access to the queen's private rooms, of which there were a dozen reserved for her private life and her servants. When the Revolution broke out, the château was not plundered, but the furniture was sold off at auctions which lasted an entire year. Some items were returned, such as the Schwerdfeger jewel-casket to the left of the bed or the fire-screen, whilst others were replaced with equivalent items: such as the seats delivered for the Countess of Provence, the queen's sister-in-law for the visit of King Gustav III of Sweden. The fabrics hanging around the bed and on the walls were re-woven in Lyons in the style of the original cartoons that had been kept. The bed and balustrade were recarved based on old documents.

THE PEERS' SALON

The antechamber under Queen Maria Theresa, it is in this room that Maria Leszczinska granted her formal audiences, sitting under a canopy. It was also there that she held her "cercle" or circle, as this formal conversation with the ladies of the court was known. Marie-Antoinette had the decoration completely changed, only retaining the ceiling paintings and for her own pleasure, the walls were adorned with apple-green damask trimmed with wide gold braid. New furniture was delivered which was both modern and refined. For the majestic commodes and corner pieces designed for this room, Riesener, the queen's favourite cabinet-maker, conformed to the latest English fashion, abandoning his habitual floral marquetry for large mahogany inlays while the gilded bronzes as well as the turquin blue plates of this majestic ensemble were matched with those of the fireplace, it too new.

THE ANTECHAMBER
FOR GRAND COUVERT REPASTS

It is in the queen's antechamber that public meals were taken, a lavish ritual which attracted quite a crowd. Only the royal family were allowed to take their seats at table. In front of them were the duchesses, princesses or high office-bearers who were privileged enough to sit on stools. There were then the other ladies and those who, by rank or with the permission of ushers, had been allowed to enter. They, however, had to stand. Louis XIV forced himself to attend this event almost every evening; for his part, Louis XV preferred a more intimate dinner with friends; as for Louis XVI and Marie-Antoinette, accounts from the period report that "The Queen sat to the left of the King. They had their backs to the fireplace [...] The King ate heartily, but the Queen kept her gloves on and did not use her napkin, which displayed very poor manners." To relieve her boredom, Marie-Antoinette requested that there should always be music in the Grand Couvert and for this purpose a platform was installed in the room for the musicians. A portrait painted by Élisabeth Vigée-Lebrun shows the Queen surrounded by her children, Madame Royale, the Dauphin and the Duke of Normandy.

◆ Silverware service created by Robert-Joseph Auguste for King George III displayed in the antechamber of the *Grand Couvert*.
◆ Élisabeth Louise Vigée-Le Brun, *Marie-Antoinette of Lorraine-Habsbourg, Queen of France and her children*, 1789. Oil on canvas, 271 × 195 cm.

At the king's table

THE SOUPER IN THE GRAND COUVERT

When at Versailles, Louis XIV always ate in public, whether for his *dîner* – our lunch, which he took alone in his bedchamber or his *souper* – our dinner – which he enjoyed with his family in a special room. When the queen and dauphine were alive, this meal was taken in the antechamber of the Grand Couvert of the Queen's Suite. As of 1690, the king continued this ritual in his first antechamber, dubbed "the Grand Couvert". Those invited to this *souper* were the king, queen, sons, daughters, grandsons and granddaughters of France. The rule was sometimes broken when the monarch wished to avoid being alone with his son, Monseigneur le Dauphin. In this case, he would invite his "bastard" offspring, much to the displeasure of Madame Palatine, his daughter-in-law. This meal was an extraordinary spectacle which hundreds of carefully chosen courtiers would stand and observe every day. Only twelve titled ladies had the right to be seated on stools before the royal table. The splendid ceremony followed the French ritual with successive presentation of five services: the *oilles* (soup) the entrées, roasted meats, fruit and dessert. The whole ceremony was a veritable ballet performed before the royal family under the guidance of the *maître d'hôtel*, baton in hand. The king had a healthy appetite and wasted little time on talking, with his sister-in-law noting on 3 February 1707: "Everyone swallowed down what was before them in silence as in a convent; only the occasional utterance was audible whispered in hushed tones to one's neighbour".

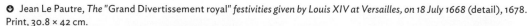

❶ Jean Le Pautre, *The "Grand Divertissement royal" festivities given by Louis XIV at Versailles, on 18 July 1668* (detail), 1678. Print, 30.8 × 42 cm.

THE QUEEN'S GUARDS ROOM

The Queen's staircase, also known as the Marble staircase, gave access to the Queen's Suite through this Guardroom in which, night and day, twelve bodyguards served the queen. At Versailles, only the king, the queen and the dauphin had a personal guard made up of soldiers belonging to these elite units which were the king's four companies of bodyguards. The next large room, known today as the "Coronation room", was allocated to them and served as the guardroom.

The Queen's Guard Room is the only room in the suite to have retained the 17th century décor: as the queen had no occasion to be there, it was never deemed necessary to modernise it. It is for this reason that the marble wall panels characteristic of the original State Apartments along with the paintings placed there in 1680, from the Jupiter Salon, which became the Salon of War, can still be seen.

⬆ Noël Coypel, *Justice punishing* (detail), 1681. Oil on plaster, south-west corner piece of the ceiling.

THE KING'S SUITE

Traditionally, the king had two apartments: a ceremonial apartment for official events and a private apartment for his personal life, but soon after the definitive installation of the Court at Versailles in 1682 and the death of Queen Maria Theresa the following year, Louis XIV had a suite of rooms designed around the Marble Courtyard which became his principal living quarters. He held both public and private events here, giving the latter a new official character. This life, which was one of perpetual performance in which every moment was governed by etiquette, was imposed upon his successors, who nevertheless had areas designed that they could retreat to. But until the end of the Ancien Régime, the King's Suite remained the power base of the crown. In its current configuration, the King's Suite comprises five rooms: a guardroom, two antechambers, the bedchamber and the council cabinet.

THE MARBLE STAIRCASE

This staircase, also known as the "Queen's staircase", was the most used by the Court as it led both to the King's Suite and the Queen's Suite and, under Louis XIV, the apartment of Madame de Maintenon, whom the King married secretly upon the death of Maria Theresa. It was built in 1681, to match the Ambassadors' Staircase located at the other side of the courtyard. The richness of the décor stems above all from its ornamental paving and panelling composed of a variety of marble. It was Colbert who had ordered the kingdom's quarries to be prospected and developed and the marble that came from them was remarkable both in terms of the quality of the raw material and the way it was worked.

⊕ After Claude Lefebvre, *Full-length portrait of Louis XIV, King of France and Navarre* (detail), *circa* 1670. Oil on canvas, 196 × 155 cm.

THE ŒIL-DE-BŒUF ANTECHAMBER

This second antechamber, following on from the Guardroom and Antechamber of the King's Grand Couvert and where courtiers waited to be admitted to the King's bedchamber, owes its name, literally "the bulls eye salon", to the oval window located in the ceiling frieze. Its dimensions and décor are the results of the renovations ordered by Louis XIV in 1701 to replace two approximately equally-sized rooms that had previously been there for seventeen years: one was a small antechamber and the other the King's bedchamber. The latter having become too small due to the number of courtiers present at his ceremonial rising in the morning, Louis XIV had it moved to its current location. The new, much bigger antechamber was decorated in a new style since Louis XIV, weary of splendour, wanted "youthfulness strewn everywhere". The ring of children adorning the frieze meets this requirement and its charm heralded the art of the 18th century. In particular, it is worth noting the painting by Jean Nocret, *The Family of Louis XIV in 1670 dressed up as mythological figures*, from the Château de Saint-Cloud.

⊙ Jean Nocret, *The Family of Louis XIV in 1670 dressed up as mythological figures, 1670*. Oil on canvas, 305 × 420 cm.

The king rises

THE RISING AND RETIRING OF THE SUN KING

At Versailles, Louis XIV imposed daily rituals for all of his activities. And this began with the rising ceremony. It was viewed as a very important moment and the king liked his court to be present in number; regular attendance was one of the main criteria for obtaining royal favour. At 8.30am every day, the first *valet de chambre* on duty, who slept by his side on a pallet bed, drew back the heavy trimmed curtains and uttered the customary phrase to the king: "Sire, it is time". The *Petit Lever* then began, setting in motion the royal procedure for welcoming the nobles and servants who entered the bedchamber one after the other. The nanny would be first to embrace the sovereign followed by the physician who would inquire as to his good health. The first gentleman of the bedchamber in years, notified by a bedchamber boy, guarded the door and served as usher. He would announce to the king those persons waiting to enter. According to their rank, the first to enter were those with the right to see the king still in his bed then, during the *Grand Lever,* those who could see him attired in a dressing gown seated in his armchair and finally the entire court who entered as he was being dressed. At the end of the ceremony, almost 150 people would, in the words of Molière, endeavour to "lay siege to the king's chair".

The same ceremony took place in the evening but in reverse. The bedchamber remained full as the sovereign greeted all of those present. Louis XIV was gradually undressed, illuminated by he who had the honour of clutching the candlestick holder. According to Saint-Simon, the granting of this distinction was proof that "the king possessed before all men the art of giving importance to trifles". Encouraged by the ushers who would cry "Advance gentlemen", the crowd slowly filed out of the room. The first *valet de chambre* would then find himself alone with the king and would lock the doors from the inside before sleeping near the king's bed.

Louis XV then Louis XVI retained the rising and retiring ceremonies, although they greatly simplified them from the time when they occupied their new bedchamber in 1738 in which they actually slept. We can therefore imagine them crossing the Council Cabinet in dressing gowns morning and night to rise and retire publicly in the grand bedchamber of Louis XIV, transformed into a ceremonial room.

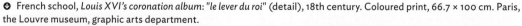

⊙ French school, *Louis XVI's coronation album: "le lever du roi"* (detail), 18th century. Coloured print, 66.7 × 100 cm. Paris, the Louvre museum, graphic arts department.

THE KING'S BEDCHAMBER

It was in 1701 that the King's Bedchamber, the genuine heart of Court life, came to be located in the centre of the château. When the king was there, access was strictly governed by etiquette, but in his absence, anyone could visit it, which astonished contemporaries. Louis XIV slept there, but his successors had another smaller bedchamber installed that was more comfortable. They did, however, continue to observe the ceremonial "Lever" (rising) and "Coucher" (retiring) rituals. Louis XIV returned to his bedchamber at around 1 o'clock in the afternoon to lunch "au petit couvert" (lesser service), in other words alone at table, but always in the presence of the men of the Court. The bedchamber was also where individual audiences were held – or ceremonial audiences for ambassadors – and swearing-in ceremonies for the highest offices. It is the only space in the château that was not transformed by his successors who kept the masterpieces of the royal collections embedded in the panelling.

The room retained its original décor after the Revolution and, in particular, some of its paintings: *The Four Evangelists* and *Caesar's Denarius* by Valentin de Boulogne, *Saint John the Baptist* by Carraciolo, *Mary Magdalene* by Dominichino, *Self Portrait* and *Portrait of the Marquis de Moncade* by Van Dyck.

THE COUNCIL CABINET

Louis XIV had two rooms here; in one, adjoining the bedchamber, the King held council daily from 11 o'clock in the morning to 1 o'clock in the afternoon: "On Sunday, and often on Monday, there was a Council of State; on Tuesday, a Finance Council; on Wednesday, a Council of State; on Saturday, a Finance Council [...]. Thursday morning was almost always blank. It was also the grand day taken advantage of by the bastards, the Batîments, the valets, etc., because the King had nothing to do. On Friday after the mass the King was with his confessor, and the length of their audiences which had no limits and might last until dinner." (Saint-Simon, *Memoirs*).

In 1755, Louis XV combined the Council Cabinet and Wig Cabinet of Louis XIV to create a single room in which the panelling, designed by Gabriel and carved by Antoine Rousseau, depicts the various government departments such as the marine department and the war department... For more than a century, all major political decisions were taken in this room, including, in 1775, France's involvement in the American War of Independence.

THE KING'S PRIVATE APARTMENTS

The King's Private Apartments and the neighbouring cabinets look out onto the Marble Courtyard and the Royal Courtyard on the right. Laid out under the reign of Louis XV, they begin with a small guardroom on the ground floor to protect access to the king's staircase. This leads to the first floor and two antechambers (the antichambre des chiens or dogs' antechamber and the dining room for returning hunting parties), a bedchamber and a large cabinet preceding a suite of rooms for specific uses. It was there that royal collections had been displayed under Louis XIV. painting cabinet, book cabinet, sea-shell cabinet as well as the small gallery decorated by Mignard, Le Brun's rival, in which the famous *Mona Lisa* by Leonardo da Vinci was kept.

LOUIS XV'S BEDCHAMBER

Not far from the large Louis XIV's bedchamber which was as impractical as it was majestic, Louis XV had a new bedchamber designed in 1738 that was smaller and south-facing, hence easier to heat. The sculptor Jacques Verbeckt designed the panelling and, in particular, the large palm trees and royal arms which decorate the alcove partition. The only modifications ordered for Louis XVI involved creating an invaluable little dressing room reached through a small door on the left and commissioning the delivery of new furniture, including the gold-embroidered half-damask reproducing the alcove hanging that could be found there in 1789.

⊙ Armand-Vincent de Montpetit, *Portrait of Louis XV* (detail), March 1774. Oil on canvas, 74 × 62 cm.

THE CLOCK CABINET

Louis XV took a keen interest in science and, in particular, astronomy. Seen here on the floor of this cabinet is the Paris meridian embodied by a copper strip. The extraordinary clock, which gave the room its name, was presented to the Academy of Sciences and then to the King in Choisy before being moved here in 1754.

In addition to the time, the clock indicates the day of the week, the month, the year and the phases of the moon; in the crystal sphere, the planets can be seen revolving around the sun. The clock designed by Passemant, the King's engineer, executed by the clockmaker Dauthiau and whose bronze case was made by Caffiéri, is an artistic and scientific monument. The crystal sphere at the top contains the sun and the planets, moving according to Copernicus' system. It was used to set the first official time throughout the kingdom.

THE KING'S INNER CABINET

This "corner cabinet", as it was commonly known, looks out onto both the Marble courtyard and the royal courtyard. Louis XV was often there and it is from the balcony that he watched, his eyes filled with tears, the departure of Madame de Pompadour's funeral procession, one winter's evening in 1764. Although it was redecorated several times during his reign, the décor of the panelling remains one of the most beautiful works of Jacques Verbeckt who carved the panels in 1753. This room had the furniture made for it, in particular the roll-top "secretary" or desk ordered from Œben in 1760 and finished by Riesener nine years later.

It was the first piece of furniture of this type and was a solution to the king's wishes to be able to leave his papers on his desk but sheltered from prying eyes. Remarkable for the beauty of its marquetry inlays and bronzes, it is also a mechanical marvel: a single quarter turn of the key simultaneously unlocked and locked the roll-top and all the drawers.

THE BATHROOM

The king's baths were amongst the last items commissioned by Louis XV. The style of the panelling, reproducing engravings evoking aquatic pleasures in medallions edged with reeds and narcissi, with matt gold, burnished gold and green gold effects, testify to a new taste. It was not Verbeckt, but his rival Antoine Rousseau, assisted by his son, who sculpted them in 1771. The bath was removed when Louis XVI installed his "pièce de la cassette" (or privy purse room) in which he kept records of his private accounts.

LOUIS XVI'S LIBRARY

This library, designed by the architect Gabriel shortly before the death of Louis XV in 1774, was one of Louis XVI's favourite rooms in which he indulged his passion for sciences and, particularly, geography. A globe of the earth carried by Atlas can be seen here, used by the king to trace the progress of great maritime adventures, especially that of La Pérouse which he had inspired and supported, as well as the large Riesener table, the top of which is made from a single piece of mahogany, 2.10 metres in diameter, and which is raised on jacks as Louis XVI needed a perfectly flat surface to mark out his corrections to geographic maps.

THE PORCELAIN DINING ROOM

This dining room, created for Louis XV in 1769 for his post-hunt suppers, was used mainly by Louis XVI and Marie-Antoinette. Over a twenty-year period, around forty guests regularly sat around the extendable table for these so-called "society" meals, a new type of meal mid-way between the great official banquets and "private" meals. If the number of guests exceeded the number of seated places, the men partook of their buffet from the billiard table in the neighbouring room. This dining room is also called the Porcelain Salon as every year at Christmas, Louis XVI had the latest items from the Sèvres manufactory displayed there.

⊙ View of Louis XVI's library.

⊙ View of the Porcelain Dining Room.

LOUIS XVI'S GAMES ROOM

Originally, Louis XIV's Cabinet of Curiosities was here, an extraordinary object of which there is no longer any trace. Having gone through various transitions, it is currently presented as it was at the time of Louis XVI when it was used as a games room. After a meal, guests withdrew there to take coffee. Louis XVI sat at a backgammon table whilst one of his brothers played billiards in the neighbouring room, the other whist. The furniture, sold in the Revolution, has largely been bought back: the four corner pieces ordered from Riesener in 1774 as well as the chairs delivered by Boulard in 1785. The works chosen by Louis XVI have also been put back on the walls: gouaches commemorating the military victories of his grandfather Louis XV, painted by Van Blarenberghe.

THE KING'S SMALL CABINETS

A year after the Court returned to Versailles in 1722, stags' heads were placed on the façades of the king's courtyard. These were made of plaster and painted to make them more colourful in the eyes of the young Louis XV, then aged thirteen. Around this courtyard, now named the Cour des Cerfs or Stags' Courtyard, a maze of rooms was developed reserved for the sovereign's use, "charming little spaces that only his confidants had access to": the king's private cabinets. The layout, use and décor of these "rats' nests" were constantly altered at no small cost according to royal whims and, under Louis XV, included a library, a cabinet for turning ivory, kitchens, distilleries, jam-making rooms, a bathroom and, on an upper terrace, aviaries, as well as reception rooms for those who were lucky enough to be granted the much coveted favour of attending post-hunt suppers. Louis XV lived there and was joined by his last mistress Madame du Barry following the death of his wife. Louis XVI had a carpentry room there, as well as a wood-turning room, an ironworks, a room for mechanics and an electricity gallery, etc.

⬆ François-Hubert Drouais, *Portrait of Madame Du Barry with flowers* (detail), 1769. Oil on canvas, 70.5 × 58 cm.
➡ View of the series of rooms in the Madame Du Barry Apartment.

Rules of etiquette

WAYS AND CUSTOMS OF THE COURT

Adopted by most royal and princely courts in Europe in the 17th century, etiquette was a series of rules and precedents intended to establish the distance separating the sovereign from his subjects. The notion reached the court of Bourgogne of Philippe le Bon in the 15th century, where it designated a formula intended to preserve the customs of the king and his entourage. Though not the instigator, Louis XIV perfected the practices which his ancestor Henri III had already imposed on his court to civilise it after the Wars of Religion. Etiquette governed the life of the court – rising in the morning, council meetings, meals, promenades, retiring at night, etc. – relations between individuals, language, the most trivial acts and gestures and all kinds of minor details such as the type of chair – with or without a backrest or armrests – to which one might accede depending on social rank, length of train, etc. Louis XIV codified it for each occasion and according to development of the interiors. It is customary to maintain that much of the etiquette disappeared with the Grand Monarch in 1715 and that it was effectively abolished as of the reign of Louix XV. Although Louis XIV-style "codes" were somewhat neglected in the 18th century, this do not necessarily lead to customs being forgotten. Rather than a slide into decadence, there was a review of the term "etiquette". By means of his reform of the King's Household - reduction in the number of servants in particular - during his reign, Louis XVI completed the deconsecration of the monarchy and royal etiquette was stripped of its original meaning.

⊙ *King Louis XIV surrounded by members of his family and princes of royal blood or The glorious and flourishing Royal family (detail), 1698. Fragment of the* Royal Almanac for the year 1699, *1698. Engraving, 43.5 × 55 cm.*

MARIE-ANTOINETTE'S PRIVATE CABINETS

On the other side of her Queen's Suite, the queen had some small rooms reserved for her own private use and that of her chambermaids. During the time of Louis XIV, Queen Maria Theresa only had an oratory and a boudoir there. Later, the queen had many more private rooms. Maria Leszczinska annexed the rooms from the main body of the building which separates the Queen's Courtyard from the Dauphin's Courtyard; she used to retire there to read, paint, meditate or receive her closest friends. Marie-Antoinette added further mezzanines and floors, to such an extent that she ended up with an entire private apartment on the ground floor looking out over the Marble Courtyard. Generally speaking, the private areas – which were bare of any official character and therefore escaped the etiquette that even dictated the exact nature of the furnishings – mirrored changes in fashion to a greater extent that the State Apartments did. This was true for both the king and the queen. However, whilst Louis XVI was often quite happy with what had been done for his grandfather Louis XV, Marie-Antoinette was forever ordering new décors and new pieces of furniture.

⊕ Élisabeth Louise Vigée-Le Brun, *Marie-Antoinette of Lorraine-Hapsburg, Archduchess of Austria, Queen of France* (detail), 18th century. Oil on canvas, 223 × 158 cm.

THE GILDED STUDY

When she was at Versailles, it was to her inner cabinet – the biggest of the queen's private rooms – that Marie-Antoinette often retired to receive her children and friends, to play music with Grétry as her teacher, or pose for Madame Vigée-Lebrun, her favourite painter. Created for Maria Leszczinska, this room was redecorated in 1783 from designs by Richard Mique, Marie-Antoinette's architect. The panelling by the Rousseau brothers, adorned with classical sphinxes and tripods, alludes to the recent discovery of Pompeii and Herculaneum. The majority of the items of furniture and objets d'art seen there today belonged to the sovereign: for example, the commode, one of Riesener's most beautiful creations, delivered for her bedchamber in Marly, and the "Chinese" Sèvres vases on top of it, which come from her apartment in Saint-Cloud.

Through a small door to the left of the fireplace, this Cabinet doré or Gilded Study – so-called due to the profusion of gold on the panelling, the bronzes, the seats – opens into a small room painted in "vernis Martin" dating from the 1750s. It is the only original example of the vogue for this process that was an imitation of Chinese lacquer. The panelling there comes from an inner cabinet of the apartment of Marie-Josèphe of Saxony located on the ground floor; it was Marie-Antoinette herself who had this décor created for her mother-in-law brought up to her own private rooms.

THE MERIDIAN CABINET

The unusual shape of this boudoir, with its cut-off corners, enabled the queen's servants to move from the main bedchamber to the other rooms without disturbing the queen who, midway through the day, would come to rest there, hence the name Meridian. It was in 1781, once Marie-Antoinette had finally given birth to an heir, that the room was given its décor of panelling, the motifs of which can also be seen in bronze appliqués on the glazed doors. The dolphin seen there evokes the child, whilst the roses, the Habsburg eagle and the peacock, associated with the goddess Juno, are allusions to the queen herself.

THE BILLIARD CABINET

The queen had other cabinets on the second floor. One of these served as the billiard room. Its silks have been restored while the sofas by J. Jacob have been replaced.

THE APARTMENTS OF THE DAUPHIN AND DAUPHINE

These ground floor apartments – which communicated directly with those of the queen located just above via several staircases – were always reserved for the leading members of the royal family. Notably, Louis XIV's brother, known as Monsieur, then his son known as Monseigneur were accommodated there. Finally his nephew, known as the Regent, who governed after his death, also lived there. Their current state corresponds to the period when they were inhabited by Louis XV's son (Louis, dauphin of France) and by his second wife Marie-Josèphe of Saxony, that is to say between 1747 and 1765. The two apartments of the Dauphin and Dauphine are connected by their last room, which is also the most intimate one: the prince's library and the princess' inner cabinet, painted in "vernis Martin". Very close, the dauphin Louis and his wife Marie-Josèphe of Saxony went their often, leaving the connecting door open. For a long time occupied by the Count and Countess of Provence, the brother and sister-in-law of Louis XVI, they sheltered the young dauphin, the future Louis XVII, and his sister Madame Royale when the Revolution broke out.

⬆ Jean-Marc Nattier, *Marie Josèphe of Saxony, Dauphine of France* (detail), 1751. Oil on canvas, 105 × 120 cm.
➡ View of the Dauphine's inner cabinet.

THE DAUPHIN'S BEDCHAMBER

From the Marble courtyard, it is possible to reach the Dauphin's Bedchamber via a Guardroom and two antechambers. The function of the room, as well as its dimensions and décor, date back to 1747. Before that time there had been a smaller room in its place, first the Cabinet doré (Gilded study) of Monseigneur who displayed his collection of paintings there, followed by the Regent's study. He was to die there in 1723. As for all the decoration work carried out during the time that he was the king's chief architect (from 1742 to 1775), Gabriel supplied the designs for this bedchamber. As was the custom, silks were hung in the alcove whilst the rest of the room was panelled with carved oak (made in Jacques Verbeckt's workshop – it was he who produced most of the panelling destined for Versailles) highlighted in white and gold, in other words, a white background with gilded motifs.

The Dauphine's bed having disappeared, it was replaced by a "duchess" bed – i.e. one in which the canopy is not held up by pillars – produced in around 1740 for the Marchioness de Créquy; its fabrics are decorated with motifs of foliage and medallions produced in petit point needlework; the needlework on the headboard depicts the sleep of the shepherd Endymion.

THE DAUPHINE'S BEDCHAMBER

It was in this bedchamber that the dauphine Marie-Josèphe of Saxony, daughter of King Augustus III of Poland and wife of Louis XV, gave birth to three future kings of France: Louis XVI, Louis XVIII and Charles X. Nothing remains of the décor it was given in 1747, with the exception of the panels over the doors painted by Jean Restout. The original bed has been replaced with a beautiful "Polish-style" bed (with a dome-shaped canopy supported by four pillars) designed by Nicolas Heurtaut. On either side of the bed are portrayed the Dauphine's sisters-in-law, Louis XV's daughters, and in particular Henriette of France as Flora and Marie-Adelaide of France as Diana, painted by Jean-Marc Nattier.

THE DAUPHINE'S STATE CABINET

After the Dauphin's apartments, those of the Dauphine are visited in reverse order to the norm in terms of the succession of rooms. In other words: first and second antechambers, state cabinet, bedchamber and finally the private cabinet. In the state cabinet, the dimensions of which date back to the time when the room served as a guardroom for Louis XIV's son, Marie-Josèphe of Saxony assembled the ladies in her entourage for conversation or games. As was the case throughout the suite, a new décor had been designed for her, but it disappeared in the 19th century on the orders of Louis-Philippe. Only the large console was spared and replaced under a mirror, the frame of which has been restored; it now supports a barometer produced for the future Louis XVI who, until his accession in 1774, occupied these apartments. On the "flame-coloured" wall covering, a modern version of that described in inventories, were hung portraits of ministers and members of the Royal family from the beginning of the reign of Louis XV.

◐ View of the Dauphine's bedchamber.

THE APARTMENTS OF MADAME VICTOIRE AND MADAME ADELAIDE

Beyond the Lower Gallery, the ladies' apartments are symmetrical to the apartments of the Dauphin and the Dauphine. They too were transformed into a museum room by Louis-Philippe and have since been restored as princes' apartments. "Mesdames", as the daughters of Louis XV were called, began moving into these apartments in 1752, but only two of them, Adélaïde and Victoire – who did not marry nor enter a convent – inhabited them until the Revolution.

MADAME VICTOIRE'S STATE CABINET

Originally, this was the octagonal cabinet of Louis XIV's Bathroom apartment, one of the most original creations of the Sun King, in which the opulence of the marbles, sculpture and paintings surpassed that of the State Apartment. In 1763, the Mesdames were given permission to have the outdated décor changed; from this renovation remains the cornice, the panelling in the corners of the room as well as the beautiful fireplace. A Blanchet harpsichord is a reminder that Madame Victoire played this instrument admirably and that Mozart dedicated his first six harpsichord sonatas to her.

⬆ Jean-Marc Nattier, *Madame Victoire de France* (detail), circa 1747. Oil on canvas, 81 × 64 cm.

MADAME ADELAIDE'S PRIVATE CABINET

This room was famous in its time as Madame de Pompadour's red lacquer cabinet. Indeed Louis XV's mistress, once she had become the king's "lady friend" in 1750, occupied what was later to become Madame Adelaide's apartment; moreover she died there in 1764. With its highly refined furniture and its souvenirs of the Château de Bellevue, the Mesdames' favourite residence, the current layout of Madame Adelaide's private cabinet is evocative of this princess who, according to the Countess of Boigne "had an extreme need for quests invented by luxury".

⬆ Jean-Marc Nattier, *Madame Adélaïde de France tying knots* (detail), 1756. Oil on canvas, 128 × 96 cm.

View of Madame Adélaïde's Private Cabinet.

View of Madame Victoire's State Cabinet.

THE CHAPEL ROYAL

Louis XIV only used this chapel for five years since it was not officially opened until 1710. The one he used the most, built in 1682 where the Hercules Salon is now located, soon proved to be too cramped. However wars delayed work on the large chapel, begun in 1689 by Hardouin-Mansart. The architect never saw the building completed as he died in 1708. After his death, his brother-in-law, Robert de Cotte, took over, but the general lines of the architecture and the décor had been fixed in 1699: a design including a nave, aisles and ambulatory, an elevation with tribunes (or vaulted galleries), a harmony of white and gold contrasting with the polychrome of the ornamental marble tiling and vault paintings; the project resulted in an original work harking back to a blend of gothic architecture and baroque aesthetics.

Every day, usually at 10 a.m., the court attended the King's Mass. The King himself would be in the royal tribune, surrounded by his family. The public occupied the side galleries and the nave. The King only attended for major religious celebrations, ceremonies of the order of the Holy Spirit, christenings and the weddings of the Children of France celebrated there from 1710 to 1789.

Above the altar, around Cliquot's organ played by grand masters such as François Couperin, the Musique de la Chapelle (Chapel music choir), famous across Europe, sang anthems throughout the daily services.

⊕ Detail of the arch of the royal chapel: Antoine Coypel, *The eternal father in his glory and groups of angels announcing the coming of the Messiah or carrying instruments of the Passion,* 1708-1710.

THE OPERA ROYAL

From the outset, Versailles provided the setting for many events but until 1770 these always took place in provisional locations. It was at this time that the large auditorium, already planned by Louis XIV and under permanent consideration, was developed hastily for the marriage celebrations of the Dauphin, the future Louis XVI, to the Archduchess of Austria, Marie-Antoinette. This event led Gabriel, assisted by the stage engineer Arnoult, to design a modular auditorium which could be used for operas as well as balls and feasts, thanks to a mechanism that allowed the floor of the auditorium to be raised to the level of the stage.

The dimensions of the auditorium, which then accommodated more than a thousand spectators and which can still house six hundred today, make it the biggest court theatre in existence. However the auditorium only represents a quarter of the whole since the stage is as deep as the auditorium and the "below stage" areas for scene changes double its height. Its elegance stems from its harmonies of blue, white and gold, but above all from the colonnade and the mirror arcades of the last floor as well as the decompartmentalisation of the boxes: Gabriel thus avoided the "chicken coop" effect characteristic of Italian theatres as a result of tiered boxes stacked one on top of the other. Built from wood for the purposes of both economy and acoustics, the entire auditorium was vaulted by one of the best carpenters, Delanois, and enhanced with motifs carved by the great sculptor, Pajou. However, this auditorium was little used since, apart from the fact that it was reserved for exceptional occasion and was therefore sometimes too large for events, it cost a small fortune in candles and ordinary events were once again usually held in a provisional room. On 1 October 1789, the opera played host to a Banquet for the King's Bodyguards, an event that was considered to be highly provocative and which was instrumental in the riot that forced the royal family to leave Versailles for good five days later. Re-used in 1837 for the inauguration of the museum created by Louis-Philippe, it temporarily housed the headquarters of the National Assembly in 1871, followed by the Senate from 1876 to 1879.

⬆ Jean-Louis Prieur, *Banquet of the bodyguards in the opera hall at Versailles, 1st October 1789* (detail), 18th century. Drawing, black ink, stump, grey wash, lead pencil, black stone, 19.5 × 25.4 cm. Paris, Carnavalet Museum, deposit of the Louvre museum, graphic arts department.

Lully, Molière, Rameau, Mozart...

ARTISTS AT VERSAILLES

Louis XIV was surrounded by artists from an early age and would bend an attentive ear to *Orfeo* by Luigi Rossi, dance alongside Jean-Baptiste Lully or discover Romanesque literature with his mistress Marie Mancini. Versailles gave him an opportunity to "invite" the arts to his home. Under the guidance of Charles Le Brun, a whole host of painters, stucco artists, sculptors and other prestigious decorators embellished the palace. As of the first modifications, writers – La Fontaine in *Les Amours de Psyché et Cupidon*, Mademoiselle de Scudéry in *La Promenade de Versailles...* – sang their praises before the official versions had even emerged. Molière put on plays for the first major celebrations while Racine became the official author of the second part of the reign. By combining ballet, music and song, Lully invented, with the librettist Philippe Quinault, French opera, also termed "lyrical tragedy" and which became the European model par excellence in the 17th century. This artistic tradition continued throughout the following reigns: Rameau triumphed with his operas before giving way to Gluck, the sculptor Bouchardon exhibited in the Hercules Salon, the painter Nattier produced portraits of the king's daughters, Mozart performed for the royal family at the age of six and the painter Hubert Robert created the groves of the Baths of Apollo. In short, Versailles showcased French know-how in all its variety.

⊙ Jean Le Pautre, *The festivities given by Louis XIV to celebrate winning back Franche-Comté, at Versailles in 1674, First day, Wednesday 7 July: performance of Quinault's opera Alceste in the Marble Courtyard of the Château de Versailles* (detail), 1676. Print, 30.8 × 42.7 cm.
⊙ Anonymous, *Royal Ballet of the Night, Louis XIV as Apollo*, 17th century. Drawing. Paris, Bibliothèque nationale de France.

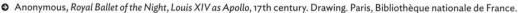

THE GARDENS AND GROUNDS

It was in the gardens that Louis XIV would give free rein to his imagination. The king who "delighted in bullying nature, taming it with art and treasures", levelling and excavating earth and major hydraulics works, successfully claimed back marshland judged to be a health risk. The main authorising officer was André Le Nôtre who raised the art of the "French style" garden to new heights. Created in the period of 1660-1680, the grounds drew on the Apollonian myth with their sculptured groups. The gardener traced it out from the long perspective of the central east-west axis – representing the sun's daytime trajectory – and the horizontal south-north axis. Le Nôtre constantly sought transparency, water effects and the unexpected blending with the different flowerbeds and groves. As of the 1680s, the gardens took on a more mineral appearance under the influence of Jules Hardouin-Mansart. At the start of his reign, Louis XV respected the work of his great-grandfather and even completed some projects. Louis XVI failed to escape the general replanting of the grounds, picking up the original outline while eliminating certain poorly kept groves and modifying the appearance of a number of avenues to bring them into line with the fashion of the day.

◐ View of the Pyramid, Ceres and Flora basins.

WEST SIDE

After the great storms of February 1990 and December 1999, the grounds were replanted and the original physiognomy of the gardens was restored. Viewers observing the gardens from the central window in the Hall of Mirrors have their eyes drawn from the Water Parterre (composed of two ornamental pools) to the horizon. Le Nôtre took pleasure in developing this original vista, that had existed prior to the reign of Louis XIV, and extending it by widening the Royal Avenue and having the Grand Canal dug.

THE WATER PARTERRE

The two ornamental pools appear to be an extension of the château's façade. Altered several times, this ensemble only acquired its definitive appearance in 1685. The sculpted décor was then designed and overseen by Charles Le Brun: each pool is ringed with four reclining statues representing the rivers of France, as well as four nymphs and four groups of children. From 1687 to 1694, the Keller brothers, foundry owners, cast the models supplied by the sculptors (Tuby, Le Hongre, Regnaudin, Coysevox, etc.) in bronze.

The Water Parterre cannot be viewed separately from the two fountains, known as the "Combats des Animaux" ("Animals in Combat"), finished in 1687, which frame the great stairway going down towards the Latona Basin, or the six allegorical statues: *L'Air* or *Air* (by Le Hongre), *Le Soir* or *Evening* (by Desjardins), *Le Midi* or *Noon* and *Le Point du Jour* or *Daybreak* (by G. Marsy), *Le Printemps* or *Spring* (by Magnier) and *L'Eau* or *Water* (by Le Gros), which formed part of Colbert's grande commande or "large order" for marble statues in 1674.

⊕ French school, *View of the Château de Versailles across the Water Parterre* circa 1675 (detail), 17th century. Oil on canvas, 136 × 154 cm.

THE LATONA BASIN

Inspired by Ovid's *Metamorphoses*, the Latona Basin illustrates the legend of Apollo's mother and Diana protecting her children from the insults of the peasants of Lycia and asking Jupiter to avenge her. This he did by turning them into frogs or lizards.

The central marble work by the Marsy brothers depicting Latona and her children was originally located, in 1670, on a rock. It was surrounded by six half-submerged frogs, and twenty-four more frogs were positioned outside the basin, on the raised lawn. At that time, the goddess looked towards the château.

This arrangement was modified by Jules Hardouin-Mansart between 1687 and 1689. The rock made way for a concentric marble plinth and the Latona group now faces the Grand Canal. The Latona Basin is extended by a parterre where the two lizard fountains are located.

◑ Gaspard and Balthasar Marsy, *Latona and her children*, 1668-1671. Group, marble.

Fountains and water games

TECHNICAL PROWESS

The creation of superb gardens embellished by spectacular fountains designed to impress visitors naturally required a considerable supply of water. Yet the site of Versailles was hardly conducive to this purpose and Louis XIV had to demonstrate considerable prowess to make it a reality. He set up a water distribution system which had to meet his demands permanently, endlessly calling on the technical skills of fountain makers and hydraulics specialists. Initially limited and founded on basic pumps and reservoirs, the system was gradually perfected with the construction of several artificial lakes around Versailles which, thanks to several overhead and underground aqueducts, had to supply water to the royal residence. With the increasing requirements, large-scale work became necessary. It was against this backdrop that the Marly machine came into being in 1681. Two men from Liège were behind it: the hydraulics engineer Arnold de Ville and the carpenter Rennequin Sualem. They planned to take water from the Seine at Bougival to supply the gardens of Marly and even those of Versailles. Despite the sums invested, the machine only managed to supply sufficient water to Marly and was gradually dismantled before being taken down in 1817. Deviation of the Eure river was another large-scale project which began in 1685. The Maintenon aqueduct –intended to surpass even the Romans in the field – was never completed and the general project, due to the War of the League of Augsbourg in 1688-1697, was shelved in 1704. Impressed by the structure, Louis XVI endeavoured to resume the project since the diversion channel was almost completed but a shortage of funds was to cut it short once again.

⊙ Anonymous, *Perspective view of the Apollo Basin and the Grand Canal with its flotilla at Versailles* (detail), *circa* 1705. Gouache, gold highlights, vellum, 12.5 × 16.5 cm.

THE ROYAL AVENUE

Also known as the "Tapis Vert" or "Green Carpet" due to the lawn running down the middle, the Royal Avenue is 335 metres long and 40 metres wide. The original layout dates back to Louis XIII, but Le Nôtre had it enlarged and enhanced with twelve statues and twelve vases (placed in symmetrical pairs). The majority of these are royal works sent by students of the Academy of France in Rome in the 17th century. On either side of the avenue, pathways give access to the groves that visitors to the gardens gradually discover as they go.

THE APOLLO BASIN
AND THE GRAND CANAL

A basin (known as the "Basin of Swans") existed at this spot as early as 1636, under Louis XIII. Louis XIV had it enlarged and adorned with the sumptuous and famous ensemble in gilded lead representing Apollo on his chariot, a work by Tuby based on a drawing by Le Brun. Tuby produced this monumental group between 1668 and 1670 at the Gobelin manufactury. It was then transported to Versailles before being put into position and gilded the following year.

Work on the Grand Canal, which is next, lasted eleven years (from 1668 to 1679). It provided the setting for numerous water festivals and countless small boats sailed on it. From 1669, Louis XIV had miniature boats and vessels brought in. In 1674, the Republic of Venice sent the king two gondolas and four gondoliers, who stayed in a group of buildings at the head of the canal, known as Little Venice.

➊ View down the Grande Perspective, the vista including the Royal Avenue, the Apollo Basin and the Grand Canal.
➋ (FOLLOWING DOUBLE PAGE) View of the *Apollo on his chariot* group by Jean-Baptiste Tuby, 1668-1670. Group, gilded lead.

NORTH SIDE

In the northern part of the gardens, the water theme dominates, probably because the naturally sloping terrain was ideal for accommodating numerous water features. But the Grotto of Tethis was also located nearby until 1684. At the time, this attracted many visitors due to the variety of its fountains and the beauty of its interior décor. The same principal as is employed along the east-west axis – a central avenue, opening up the view, and lined with groves surrounded by arbours – is used here. Steps, a Pyramid fountain (equivalent to the Latona Basin), a Water Avenue (which extends the vista in the same way as the Royal Avenue) and the Dragon Basin (the theme of which can be compared with the Baths of Apollo), culminating in a vast pool of water: the Neptune Basin.

⬆ Étienne Allegrain, *Promenade by Louis XIV with view over the North Parterre in the gardens of Versailles* circa *1688* (detail), 17th century. Oil on canvas, 234 × 295 cm.

THE NORTH PARTERRE

From the central terrace and the Water Parterre, visitors go down a few steps framed by two bronze sculptures: *The Chaste Venus*, by Coysevox, and *The Knifegrinder*, by Foggini, towards the North flowerbed designed in 1664. On either side of the central avenue are the two "Bassins des Couronnes" or "Crown Basins" in which lead tritons and mermaids – works by Tuby and Le Hongre – can be seen swimming. The North Parterre is surrounded by eighteen sculptures, fifteen of which date from the grande commande or "large order" of 1674. Its iconographic design by Charles Le Brun, illustrates the myth of Apollo and his life-giving and influential race around the earth; the statues were arranged in fours: the four continents, the four seasons, the four temperaments... but the perpetual changes that were made to the way the gardens were laid out soon led to this ensemble being dispersed.

⬆ After Antoine Coysevox, *The crouching Venus or modest Venus*, 1688. Bronze.

THE PYRAMID FOUNTAIN

A work by Girardon based on a drawing by Le Brun, the Pyramid Fountain took three years to complete. It is made up of four superimposed marble basins held up by lead tritons, dolphins and crayfish.

THE FOUNTAIN OF NYMPHS' BASIN

Fed by water from the Pyramid fountain, the cascade, known as the Bain des Nymphes de Diane or Bath of Diana's Nymphs, is adorned with bas-reliefs, the most well-known of which on the supporting wall is a lead work by Girardon (1668-1670) that was previously gilded. The others are by Le Gros, Le Hongre and Magnier.

⊙ François Girardon, *The Bath of the Nymphs*, 1668-1670. Relief, lead.

⊙ François Girardon, *The Pyramid Fountain*, 17th century. Marble, lead.

The great royal entertainments

FESTIVITIES

Versailles owed its reputation not only to its gardens but also the festivities which took place there. Louis XIV used it as the backdrop for all of his entertaining. As of 1665, Madame de Motteville, a confidante of the queen mother, Anne of Austria, wrote of Versailles and Louis XIV: "It was the theatre of his pleasures and intended to serve his own magnificence, whose treasures illustrated what a grand prince who scrimps on nothing for his own satisfaction can achieve". When the great lords amused themselves, they were able to forget revolts and cliques. Though not the only festivities of the reign, there were three major celebrations. Keen to present his first redevelopments to the court which for too long had been starved of frivolity after his marriage, between 7 and 13 May 1664, the sovereign organised the Pleasures of the Enchanted Isle. A carousel, ballets, refreshments, a *course de bagues* game on horseback, comedies and other festivities took place in the gardens where the king, like an ordinary citizen, received the greatest of the kingdom who had come to test themselves like knights of the Middle Ages. The heroine of the Great royal entertainment of 18 July 1668 was Madame de Montespan, his new mistress, although it officially commemorated the Treaty of Aix-la-Chapelle which marked the end of the Franco-Spanish war. In 1674, during the two months of summer, festivities took place celebrating the reconquest of Franche-Comté and where *Alceste* de Lully and Quinault was performed in the marble courtyard. Louis XV and Louis XVI perpetuated the tradition with births and marriages giving rise to extravagant celebrations. The birth of the dauphin in 1729 was celebrated by two large firework displays; his wedding in 1745 gave rise to major celebrations - construction of temporary theatres, the Yew Tree Ball, so called because Louis XV danced, in the company of other lords, disguised as a tree. At the wedding of the future Louis XVI with the archduchess Marie-Antoinette in 1770, the intention was to recreate the festivities of the Sun King: a feast was thus organised at the Opera on 16 May, a performance of *Persée* by Lully on 18 May, a masquerade ball and firework display followed by illumination of the Grand Canal on 19 May.

🔽 Israël Silvestre, "Les Plaisirs de l'Île enchantée" *festivities given by Louis XIV at Versailles* (detail), 1664. Print, 28.5 × 42.8 cm.

THE WATER AVENUE

According to his brother Charles – the famous fable writer – it was the architect Claude Perrrault who designed this avenue, also known as the allée des Marmousets or Children's Alley. It is ponctuated by twenty-two bronze sculptures supporting Languedoc marble basins.

THE DRAGON BASIN

The Water Avenue culminates with a half-moon at the Dragon Basin, depicting one of the episodes in the legend of Apollo: the Python (killed by the young Apollo's arrow) is surrounded by dolphins and cupids armed with bow and arrows, riding on swans. The main water jet rises up twenty-seven metres. On either side of this basin, alleys lead to two recently restored groves: to the east is the Bosquet de la France Triomphante or Triumphant France Grove and to the west the Bosquet des Trois-Fontaines or Three Fountains Grove.

⊘ View down the Water Avenue towards the Dragon Basin.
⊙ Tony Noël, after Gaspard and Balthasar Marsy, *The Dragon*, 1889. Group, gilded lead.

THE NEPTUNE BASIN

It was Le Nôtre who oversaw construction of the Neptune Basin between 1679 and 1681, at the time known as the "Pool under the Dragon" or "Fir pool". Jacques-Ange Gabriel altered it slightly in 1736 and, in 1740, fulfilling the wish of Louix XIV, the three groups of sculptures were put into place: *Neptune and Amphitrite* by L.-S. Adam, *Proteus* by Bouchardon and *Ocean*, by Lemoyne. The new basin, inaugurated by Louis XV, was admired for the number, size and variety of fountains, creating an extraordinary hydraulic ensemble.

◗ Lambert-Sigisbert and Nicolas Sébastien Adam, *Neptune and Amphitrite*, 1735-1741. Group, lead.

SOUTH SIDE

THE SOUTH PARTERRE

The best view of this is probably to be gained from the Queen's Suite, on the first floor of the château. Previously named the Flower Parterre or Love Parterre, it is located below the Orangery built by Jules Hardouin-Mansart. It is reached via a set of steps flanked by two of the oldest sculptures in the park: *Les Enfants aux sphinx* or *Children with Sphinxes*. The bronze children were modelled by Sarazin, cast by Duval in 1668 and placed on marble sphinxes, carved by Lerambert.

⬆ Jean-Baptiste Martin the Elder, *View of the Orangerie, the 100-step staircase and the Château de Versailles circa 1695 (detail)*, 17th century. Oil on canvas, 115 × 165 cm.

THE ORANGERY

Built by Jules Hardouin-Mansart between 1684 and 1686 to replace the small orangery erected by Le Vau in 1663, it comprises a central vaulted gallery, 150 metres long, extended by two side galleries beneath the Great 100-Step Staircase. Light floods in through large, arched windows. The Orangery Parterre extends over 3 ha; under Louis XIV it was adorned with a few sculptures which are now in the Louvre. Made up of four areas of lawn and a circular pool, in the summer it boasts 1,055 trees in tubs (palm trees, oleanders, pomegranate trees, eugenia, orange trees, etc.) which are housed inside the Orangery in the winter.

Beyond the Orangery Parterre, on the other side of the Route de Saint-Cyr, lies the Pool of the Swiss Digging began in 1678 and was completed in 1688. It is 682 metres long and 234 wide, covering an area of 16 ha (twice the size of the Place de la Concorde in Paris).

THE AVENUES AND GROVES

THE BACCHUS AND SATURN AVENUE

Under the reign of Louis XIV, the gardens at Versailles had fifteen bosquets or groves, in other words spaces that were hidden from view by arbours and closed off with gates. They acted as a counterpoint to the rigid regularity of the overall layout of the gardens, their décor and shape differed and their overall effect was to surprise visitors through their diversity. The majority of them were created by Le Nôtre, but some were modified by Jules Hardouin-Mansart. These charming green spaces, havens of fantasy, abound with fountains and sculptures. Festivities, dancing, music, theatre and meals were all held there. However, due to the fact that they were expensive and difficult to maintain, some groves deteriorated rapidly and were closed from as early as the 18th century. One of the most famous, the Labyrinth, was destroyed when the gardens were replanted in the period 1775-1776, others such as the Baths of Apollo were transformed in the highly fashionable Anglo-Chinese style under the reign of Louis XVI and Marie-Antoinette. In the 19th century, under the reign of Louis XVIII, the Royal Island was filled in and became the King's Garden, planted with rare and exotic trees.

⊙ François Girardon, *Saturn*, 1672-1678. Group, polychromed and gilded lead.
⊙ Gaspard and Balthasar Marsy, *Bacchus*, 1672-1678. Group, polychromed and gilded lead.

THE QUEEN'S GROVE

This grove replaced the famous Labyrinth which illustrated thirty-nine Aesop's fables at each of its crossroads by lead fountains painted au naturel depicting animals. Constructed in 1669 from an idea by Charles Perrault, it was destroyed when the gardens were replanted in the period 1775-1776, to be replaced by the Queen's Grove. The current sculptures were put in place at the end of the 19th century.

THE BALLROOM GROVE

Designed by Le Nôtre between 1680 and 1683, the Ballroom is also known as the Bosquet des Rocailles (Rockery Grove) due to the millstones and shells brought back from the African coasts and Madagascar over which the water flows. An easily accessible marble "island" in the middle was used for dancing, something Louis XIV was famous for. The musicians positioned themselves above the waterfall and the spectators would sit opposite, in an amphitheatre with grass-covered terraces.

◔ View of the Ballroom Grove.

⊕ View of the King's Garden

THE DAUPHIN'S GROVE AND THE GIRANDOLE GROVE

The Dauphin's Grove and the Girandole's Grove replace, to the north and the south, the former zigzag patterns planted under Louis XVI. Each of these groves is decorated with items ordered by Superintendent Foucquet for his château de Vaux-le Vicomte and produced in Rome based on Poussin's models and purchased from his descendants. At the end of the 17th century, the sculptor Théodon completed this series of sculptures, dedicated to the seasons or mythological divinities.

THE KING'S GARDEN

The Mirror Basin was at the edge of a large pond known as the Île d'Amour (Love Island) or Île Royale (Royal Island) (1674) on which model warships were tested out. It was not maintained during the period of the Revolution and was removed in 1817 by the architect Dufour, on the orders of Louis XVIII, to be replaced with the King's Garden. This enclosed, English-style garden was planted with superb plant species most of which were subsequently wiped out by the winter storm of 1999. All that now remains of the original design is the Mirror Basin.

THE CHESTNUT GROVE

Arranged between 1680 and 1683, it was then known as the Galerie des Antiques (Classical Gallery) or Galerie d'Eau (Water Gallery) and comprised a central avenue lined with orange trees, pruned yew trees, pools and water jets. Around this avenue there were twenty-four Classical statues. Entirely re-designed in 1704, this grove then became the Salle des Marronniers or Chestnut Grove, adorned with eight Classical busts and two statues. The only aspects of the original décor to survive are the two round basins located at each end.

THE COLONNADE GROVE

Built from 1685 by Jules Hardouin-Mansart, the Colonnade replaced a grove created by Le Nôtre in 1679: the Bosquet des Sources or Grove of Springs. This peristyle has a diameter of 32 metres; thirty-two Ionic order marble columns connected to thirty-two Languedoc marble pilasters, support arcades and a white marble cornice, itself topped by thirty-two urns. The triangular tympanums between the arches are decorated with bas-reliefs depicting children. The archstones are adorned with nymphs and naiads. In the centre, a circular marble plinth acts as a pedestal for the famous composition executed between 1678 and 1699 by Girardon: *Pluto abducting Proserpine* (a cast replaced the original, now in storage).

Saint-Simon reported Le Nôtre's reaction to this new grove: "He remained tight-lipped before the Colonnade but pressed for his view by the King he retorted: "Well Sire, if you really want my opinion. You have made a gardener of a builder (meaning Mansart) and he has duly served you a dish from his profession".

◎ View of the Chestnut Grove.
◎ View of the Colonnade with, in the centre, *the Abduction of Proserpine* by François Girardon, 1675-1695. Group, marble.

THE FLORA AND CERES AVENUE

Symmetrical to the Bachus and Saturn Basins, the Flora and Ceres Basins symbolise the summer and the spring respectively. Flora, half-naked, is resting on a bed of flowers, also surrounded by Cupids weaving garlands. The sculptor produced these between 1672 and 1677. Ceres, sickle in hand, surrounded by Cupids is reclining on the ground strewn with ears of wheat. This work is by the sculptor Regnaudin.

⬆ Jean-Baptiste Tuby, *Flora and four cupids*, 1672-1679.
Group, polychromed and gilded lead.

THE DOME GROVE

Frequently redesigned, the name of this grove has been changed each time modifications have been made. Created by Le Nôtre in 1675, it became known as the Bosquet de la Renommée or Fame Grove, in the period 1677-1678, due to the statue of La Renommée (or Fame) placed in the centre of the basin at this time with a fountain coming out of her trumpet. Between 1684 and 1704, the sculpted groups from the Apollo baths were placed there, hence the name Baths of Apollo during that period. In 1677, Jules Hardouin-Mansart built two white marble pavilions surmounted by domes, giving it its current name, although these constructions were destroyed in 1820.

THE ENCELADUS BASIN

The Enceladus Fountain was produced in lead by Gaspard Marsy between 1675 and 1677. The subject is borrowed from history from the fall of the Titans, buried beneath the rocks of Mount Olympus that they wanted to climb in defiance of Jupiter's ban on doing so. The sculptor represented a giant, half-engulfed beneath the rocks, battling against death.

THE OBELISK

The Obelisk Fountain was built by Jules Hardouin-Mansart in 1704 at the location of the former Salle des Festins (Feast Room) or Salle du Conseil (Council Room), designed by Le Nôtre in 1671. The lead décor was then used as ornamentation for the basins in the Grand Trianon garden.

⬋ Gaspard Marsy, *Enceladus*, 1675-1676. Group, gilded lead.

THE CHILDREN'S ISLAND

On the north side of the gardens, between the Rond vert or Green Circle (formerly known as the Bosquet du Théâtre d'eau or Water Theatre Grove) and the Star (formerly the Bosquet de la Montagne d'eau or Water Mountain Grove), away from the busy avenues, is hidden a circular basin from the middle of which rises a rock. This is the Children's Island, a masterpiece of purity created by Hardy in 1710. On the rock, there are six children playing with flowers, whilst two others are frolicking in the water.

THE THREE FOUNTAINS GROVE

Created by le Nôtre in 1677, this grove is the only one mentioned on an old map as being "the King's idea". It comprises three terraces, each of which presents a different basin. It was restored in 2005 to fully reveal the splendour of the composition and water jets commissioned by the sovereign: in the lower basin, the jets of water form fleurs de lys, in the centre, vertical lances and an arc of water and, finally the upper basin comprising a column of water formed by 140 jets; it is actually this imposing column that feeds the lower basins. Although hidden by trelliswork, the grove had been designed in such a way that the ageing king could go there in his bath chair and move from one place to another on lawned access ramps.

⊙ View of the Three Fountains Grove.

THE BATHS OF APOLLO

Here, a grove, known as Le Marais (the Marsh), was created during the reign of Louis XIV, between 1670 and 1673, on the instigation of Madame de Montespan. In 1704, Jules Hardouin-Mansart designed a new grove for this location to receive the *Chevaux du Soleil* or *Sun Horses* (work by Guérin and the Marsy brothers) and *Apollon servi par les Nymphes* or *Apollo tended by Nymphs* (work by Girardon and Regnaudin). This ensemble was sculpted between 1664 and 1672 to adorn the famous Grotto of Tethis and when the latter was destroyed to make way for the north wing of the Château, it was transferred to the Dome Grove.

Hardouin-Mansart designed this location therefore to showcase his outstanding works. They were sheltered under gilded lead baldaquins and placed on a plinth along the edge of a basin.

This arrangement remained in place until 1776. Then, a year after the order given by Louis XVI to replant the grounds, the painter Hubert Robert was asked to come up with a new design. The grove he created, completed in 1778, is in the then highly fashionable Anglo-Chinese style. It is his design that still remains to this day. Casts have replaced the originals which are in safe storage.

⊕ View of three groups forming the Apollo Baths nestling in the grotto with, on the left, *Sun Horses* by Gaspard and Balthasar Marsy, in the centre, *Apollo tended by nymphs* by François Girardon and Thomas Regnaudin and, on the right, *Sun Horses* by Gilles Guérin, 1667-1675. Groups, marble.

THE WATER THEATRE GROVE

Created between 1671 and 1674 by André Le Nôtre for the feasts of Louis XIV, the grove was designed as a leafy theatre with a raised part for the actors, and stands for the audience. It was composed of a multitude of fountains, the water effects of which played with the verdant architecture and trellises.

It was destroyed in 1775 under the reign of Louis XVI and gave way to an arrangement of paths and lawns. This new design is what has long inspired its name as the Bosquet du Rond Vert (the grove of the green circle).

In 2003, as part of a park replanting project, the boundary trees were renewed.

In 2015, a new Water Theatre was inaugurated thanks to landscaper Louis Benech and artist Jean-Michel Othoniel. Their contemporary creation has given new life to the grove: water features with arabesque fountains in ornate Murano glass, evoking Louis XIV's dance steps.

⊙ Fountain sculpture by Jean-Michel Othoniel, grove by Louis Benech, 2015.
⊙ François Girardon and Thomas Regnaudin, Apollo tended by nymphs, 1667-1675. Group, marble.

TRIANON, A VERY PRIVATE ESTATE

The haven of peace which the Trianon estate now represents is the result of successive expropriations and consolidations. A village named Trianon, which Louis XIV gradually bought up, used to lie on this land. After demolishing it in 1668, the sovereign asked Le Vau to build him a small pavilion. The many sculptures in Delft earthenware making it up earned it the name of "the Porcelain Trianon". Due to its fragile nature as well as its initial purpose – a lovenest for the king and Madame de Montespan – this initial château was replaced by the Grand Trianon. Disenchanted with the regulated lifestyle which he nonethless imposed on his court within the palace, the Grand Monarch viewed it a means of escaping the straightjacket of etiquette. It therefore became a reserved estate par excellence. The monarque reportedly once proclaimed "I created Versailles for my court, Marly for my friends and Trianon pour myself." With the construction of the Petit Trianon, the estate retained this particular status of a private residence in the 18th century.

◑ View of the Petit Trianon.

THE GRAND TRIANON

The Grand Trianon is located to the north-west of the château de Versailles, on the site of a former village purchased by the sovereign. Unique in terms of the originality of its architecture, it stands out as the work of Hardouin-Mansart and the king himself as Louis XIV closely oversaw its development in 1687. During this period, Versailles was crowded with courtiers. The Trianon was to be a place to rest, a private space, reserved for concerts, celebrations and even light meals, to which Louis XIV wanted to invite only the ladies of the court; later it was for family use. At this time, the Grand Trianon was known as the Marble Trianon, due to the Rance columns of the portico and the pink Languedoc pilasters, adorned with white Carrara capitals giving emphasis to all the façades, and also in contrast to a first house known as the Porcelain Trianon, the existence of which was short-lived. The Trianon is the Floral palace: from every room there is a view onto the gardens, which here are entirely given over to flowers, with a large number of varieties selected for their colours as well as their scents: "The tuberoses cause us to abandon the Trianon every evening", writes Madame de Maintenon in a letter of 8 August 1689, "men and women feel ill, overwhelmed by the scents." And all the décors, paintings and carvings on the panelling are inspired by this floral motif.

⬆ Pierre Denis Martin, *View of the Château du Grand Trianon from the Avenue in 1723* (detail), 18th century. Oil on canvas, 137 × 155 cm.
➡ View of the peristyle of the Grand Trianon.

THE MIRROR ROOM

With its wonderful view over the Grand Canal and its décor of mirrors, this room is the most beautiful in the south wing. It was the last room in the apartments that Louis XIV occupied in this part of the château between 1691 and 1703, in which he held counsel. Like the majority of the areas in the Trianon, it has retained its original décor but not the furniture, which was sold during the Revolution and later replaced by Napoleon. From 1810 to 1814, it was used as the State Cabinet of Archduchess Marie-Louise, the great-niece of Marie-Antoinette and the emperor's second wife.

THE EMPRESS' BEDCHAMBER

This room met with the same fate as the previous one. The bedchamber of Louis XIV, it has retained its décor characterised by the presence of Corinthian columns dividing the room and the wonderfully carved mosaics of the panelling. Later it was the Empress Marie-Louise's bedchamber and was re-furnished for her as it is seen today; the only exception is the bed, which was Napoleon's bed in the Tuileries Palace and the one in which his successor Louis XVIII, Louis XVI's brother, died in 1824, before finally being brought here for the last occupant of the room, Queen Marie-Amélie, King Louis-Philippe's wife.

THE LORDS' ROOM

This room has retained its original name, from the time the entire south wing was used for serving light meals. It then became the king's first antechamber, followed by that of the empress. The great table was produced in 1823 by Félix Rémond, its top being of a single piece of teak with a diameter of 2.77 m.

View of the Mirror Room.

⬆ View of the Empress' Bedchamber.

⬇ View of the Lords' Room.

THE PERISTYLE

Incorrectly called the peristyle – but the name dates from the time of Louis XIV – this portico cutting through the centre of the building gives the Grand Trianon its transparency and hence originality, allowing imperceptible passage from the courtyard to the gardens.

THE ROUND ROOM

This hall gave access to the first apartment occupied by Louis XIV for just three years, from 1688 to 1691. Its décor of Corinthian columns as well as its marble paving and paintings date from this period. To the right of the fireplace, a wooden swing door conceals the staircase used by musicians to access the gallery leading to the following room, in which the king's "souper" was taken.

⊙ View of the Round Room.

LOUIS-PHILIPPE'S FAMILY ROOM

This large room was created by Louis-Philippe from two existing rooms. In the evenings, the king and his family, who liked to stay at the Trianon, gathered in this room furnished in the spirit of the time: games and work tables, lined seats and sofas covered with yellow purl with a blue motif.

THE MALACHITE ROOM

This grand room of the Emperor took its name from the malachite gifts given by Tsar Alexander I to Napoleon that were placed there.

THE EMPEROR'S MAP ROOM

Originally this cabinet opened onto the Bosquet des Sources or Grove of Springs, a small wood, criss-crossed by streams meandering through the trees and the last creation of Le Nôtre that disappeared under Louis XVI. It then led to Madame de Maintenon's apartment and views of the gardens at Versailles, in which an elderly Louis XIV is depicted in a bath chair, are embedded in its panelling dating from 1713. In 1810, Napoleon turned this room into his map room and used the neighbouring suite of rooms as his private apartments.

THE EMPEROR'S BEDCHAMBER

The Emperor's bedchamber, one of the five rooms in his private apartments, had been decorated under Louis XV with the panelling that has survived until today. It was re-furnished in its Empire style including the beautiful "lemon-wood" moire fabrics with lilac and silver brocade border, which had been woven in Lyons for Joséphine in 1807 and which were re-used here for Napoleon in 1809. It was in December of the same year that Napoleon stayed in this private suite for the first time, just after his divorce from Josephine. The latter's

daughter, Queen Hortense, recounted, however, that the Emperor received them on the 25th of the same month: "[He] went to Trianon and asked us to visit him. I accompanied my mother. This meeting was touching. The Emperor wanted her to stay to dine. As usual, he sat opposite her. Nothing seemed to have changed [...] There was a deep silence. My mother couldn't eat anything else and I saw that she was ready to faint. The Emperor wiped his eyes two or three times without saying a word and we left immediately after dinner."

⊙ View of the Emperor's Bedchamber.

THE BEDCHAMBER OF THE QUEEN OF THE BELGIANS

The right wing, which looks over the Courtyard of Honour, housed a theatre under Louis XIV, then, under Louis XV, reception rooms (games room, dining room and a buffet room). Louis-Philippe transformed it to create apartments for his son-in-law and his daughter Louise-Marie of Orleans, the King and Queen of the Belgians. Amongst the items of furniture brought from the Tuileries Palace was the Empress Josephine's bed.

THE GAMES ROOM

Although annexed to the young Belgian sovereigns' apartments, Louis XV's former games room has retained its curved appearance and panellings as well as its beautiful purple breccia fireplace.

⊙ View of the Bedchamber of the Queen of the Belgians.

THE COTELLE GALLERY

Judiciously built to shelter the Trianon flower beds from the rigours of winter, this gallery has eleven French windows on the south side, and only five windows on the north side. It is adorned with twenty-four paintings (twenty-one of which are by Jean Cotelle) which depict the groves at Versailles and Trianon at the time they were commissioned, in 1687, precious illustrations of the gardens as they were during the 17th century. Originally, the recesses contained sofas and Louis-Philippe had the two Languedoc marble wine coolers from Louis XV's sideboards put there. It was here, on 4 June 1920, that the peace treaty with Hungary was signed, putting an end to the First World War.

THE GARDEN ROOM

At the end of the Cotelle Gallery, the Garden Room looks out over the Trianon's Salle des Marroniers or Chestnut Grove and, beyond the upper parterre, onto the transverse arm of the Grand Canal. Under Louis XIV, there was a table for the portico game (similar to roulette) placed in the centre of this room, which was subsequently replaced by a billiard table.

◔ View of the Cotelle Gallery.
◑ Jean Cotelle the Younger, *View of the Grand Trianon from the parterres, with Flora and Zephyr*, 18th century. Oil on canvas, 201 × 139 cm.

THE TRIANON-SOUS-BOIS WING

Twenty years after its construction, the Trianon had grown too small to accommodate all of Louis XIV's family. To satisfy the king, Jules Hardouin-Mansart, shortly before his death in 1708, built this Trianon-sous-Bois wing, the sobriety and elegance of which heralded the style of the 18th century. This section of the building, the only part with an upstairs, offers a set of apartments that were initially used by Madame Palatine, the king's sister-in-law, and her children.

⊙ After Pierre Paul Prud'hon, *Assumption of the Virgin Mary* (detail), 19th century. Stained glass window from the Sèvres manufactory placed above the chapel's altar.

THE CHAPEL

Alongside the garden room and its portico game, the chapel was created by Louis-Philippe on the site of Louis XIV's Billiard room for the wedding of his second daughter, Princess Marie, to Duke Alexander of Würtemberg, on 17 October 1837. The columns around the altar come from the Dome Grove while the stained glass window was commissioned from the Sèvres Manufactury and represents *The Assumption of the Virgin Mary* after Pierre-Paul Prud'hon.

THE GENERAL'S OFFICE

Between 1962 and 1967, General de Gaulle had the Trianon-sous-Bois wing restored to accommodate presidents of the French Republic. In particular, the general's office is there.

THE PETIT TRIANON

Madame de Pompadour, who wanted to "relieve the king's boredom" – she was no longer his mistress but remained a friend – was the instigator of this small château built by Gabriel between 1763 and 1768 close to the botanic garden and the new menagerie, as Louis XV was interested in the sciences. To delight the marchioness who always liked to keep up with the latest fashions, the king's architect broke away from the rococo style of aesthetics and adopted a cubic form for the building with very pure lines in keeping with the new, so-called "Greek" style that was in vogue. Its simplicity is only an outward appearance as each of the façades is different, treated according to the space it looks onto: the courtyard, the French garden with its pretty pavilion, the botanic garden and the flower garden. The same modern style can be found inside. Madame de Pompadou did not live to see the château completed (she died in 1764) and today it is mainly Marie-Antoinette's memory that lingers: in 1774, Louis XVI gave the Trianon estate to his wife who was able to live her life there removed – too far-removed for some people – from the Court.

⊙ Élisabeth Louise Vigée-Le Brun, *Queen Marie-Antoinette with a rose* (detail), 1783. Oil on canvas, 113 × 87 cm.

THE PUBLIC SALON

Devoted to games, conversation and music, this first-floor room with its sober décor gives an accurate impression of the quest for pleasure characteristic of the 18th century. The over-door paintings inspired by Ovid's *Metamorphoses* illustrate the importance given to flowers at the Trianon. They depict: *Clytia transformed into a sunflower* and *Apollo and Hyacinth*, by Nicolas-René Jollain; *Adonis changed into an anemone* and *Narcissus changed into the flower of the same name*, by Nicolas-Bernard Lépicié. The ostrich egg placed in the centre of the pedestal table comes from the collections of Madame Adelaide, one of Louis XV's daughters.

THE QUEEN'S THEATRE

Whereas the Versailles opera is a court theatre, the small auditorium at Trianon is a society theatre, as existed at the time in many country residences where, to pass the time, manor owners and their guests put on plays and operas. In her childhood in Vienna, Marie-Antoinette grew used to these informal events. She wanted to do the same thing for her family, princes of the royal family and a few close friends. In 1780, therefore, on her orders, Richard Mique built this theatre with its severe exterior and starkly contrasting refined interior which, through its blue, white and gold harmonies, brings to mind the Versailles opera, only smaller as here just 250 people could be admitted: servants on the parterre and guests upstairs behind the boxes fitted with bars. The greatest luxury does not lie in the wooden auditorium painted in false white veined marble and adorned with pasteboard sculptures but in the machinery by Pierre Boullet used for scene changes, which has fortunately been preserved. At the Trianon, plays by fashionable authors were staged – Sedaine, Rousseau – and entire operas were sung in which, everyone agreed, the queen was extremely accomplished.

THE FRENCH PAVILION

This building was called the "French" pavilion due to its location in the middle of one of these formal gardens which began to be termed "French" in contrast with the emerging fashion for English gardens. Built by Gabriel in 1750, it was one of Louis XV's first creations at Trianon, the estate of which he had cherished memories from his childhood. It comprises a vast circular salon flanked by four small rooms used as a boudoir, a rechauffoir or room for warming up food, a kitchen and a wardrobe. Accompanied by the Marchioness de Pompadour, the king often came here to rest or listen to music after a stroll through the botanic gardens or a light meal in the neighbouring Salon Frais (Cool Salon).

THE ROCK PAVILION

Overlooking the lake, this charming octagonal music pavilion was built by Richard Mique in 1777. The outside is decorated with sculptures by Deschamps: a frieze of a garland of fruits formerly coloured, pediments depicting the pleasures of hunting and gardening, window imposts symbolising the four seasons. Inside, the circular room is paved with a marble mosaic and its walls are adorned with fine arabesques.

Claude-Louis Chatelet, *Illumination of the Belvedere pavilion and the Rock* (detail), 1781. Oil on canvas, 59 × 80 cm.

THE TEMPLE OF LOVE

This Temple of Love that the queen could see from her bedchamber at the Petit Trianon was built by Richard Mique in 1778 in a neoclassical style. Entirely in marble, this precious building is above all remarkable for the quality of its Deschamps sculptures adoring its Corinthian capitals, its friezes and the inside of its dome. This exceptional quality can be explained by the fact that it was intended to house a recognised master-piece of French sculpture, *Cupid making a bow out of the club of Hercules* by Bouchardon. The original, today in the Louvre, was replaced by a copy by Mouchy, another great sculptor of the 18th century.

THE QUEEN'S HAMLET

This village with its thatched roofs, inspired by the hamlets of Normandy, was created by Mique between 1783 and 1785. Fashion demanded a "return to nature" and the queen yielded to this vogue. There were twelve houses. Facing the artificial lake, the biggest construction was the queen's cottage linked to the Billiard house by a gallery of wood, from where the Lady of the Trianon could watch the work in the fields. Behind their rustic appearance, the interiors were highly sophisticated - furniture by Riesener and Jacob, Sèvres porcelain. The Malborough tower overlooks the fishing weir as well as the milking dairy used for cheese making. Today, the water mill, the rechauffoir (or warming room), the boudoir, the dovecote and the guard's house remain of this fantasy, as well as, slightly separate, the farm which was tended by a couple of peasants from the Touraine. There was a barn - also used as a ballroom - and a butter and cheese-making dairy, of which only traces of the foundations remain.

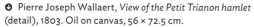

◉ Pierre Joseph Wallaert, *View of the Petit Trianon hamlet* (detail), 1803. Oil on canvas, 56 × 72.5 cm.

By order of the queen

MARIE-ANTOINETTE AT TRIANON

By offering her Trianon, Louis XVI granted her full enjoyment of the Petit Trianon. On this occasion, he reportedly told her: "Madame, since you like flowers. I wish to offer you a bouquet in the shape of Trianon". The sovereign made it her private estate where she would take her closest companions then her children, freely issuing texts stipulating "By order of the queen". The somewhat maladroit wording shocked her peers. Marie-Antoinette and the company she invited there – so stirring jealousies - lived in this residence in all simplicity, far from the stuffy etiquette of Versailles. Trianon reminded her of her childhood in Vienna; a courtier even made allusions to a "little Vienna", an unfortunate reference which was rapidly ascribed to the queen, henceforth dubbed the "Austrian". Faced with the secluded lifestyle of the queen, the public - like those excluded from Trianon - took to backbiting and openly cast doubts over the morality of the queen's society or even Marie-Antoinette herself. Although these criticisms were largely unfounded, she was rightly reproached for spending lavishly on redevelopment of the surroundings of the estate under the guidance of her architect Richard Mique, most notably by creating an English-style garden on the former botanical garden of Louis XV, a private theatre and a hamlet, which was in keeping with the fashion of the day to draw closer to nature.

⊙ Louis Nicolas de Lespinasse, *View of the Cupid Temple in the English garden of the Petit Trianon* (detail), 1780. Watercolour, gouache, 21.5 × 35 cm.
⊙ Eugène Battaille, after Adolf Ulrik Wertmuller, *Marie-Antoinette of Austria, Queen of France, and her first two children, 1868*. Oil on canvas, 275 × 188 cm.

THE HISTORY OF FRANCE MUSEUM

After the revolution of 1830 which unseated Charles X, the youngest brother of Louis XVI and the last of the Bourbons to reign, his cousin, Louis-Philippe d'Orléans was proclaimed King of the French. By a decision taken in 1833, the new sovereign demonstrated his determination to break away from the Ancien Régime by stripping Versailles of its royal residence status and transforming it into a museum. A history enthusiast at a time when the discipline was becoming a veritable science, he decided to assemble there all the painted, carved, drawn and engraved images illustrating events or personalities from French history, right from its earliest days. To achieve this, he gathered items from royal, princely, private and institutional collections and supplemented these with thousands of copies and retrospective works commissioned from contemporary artists. He had his architect Nepveu organise everything. The architect went on to destroy many princely apartments, especially in the main two wings of the château where these history galleries are still in place today. Whilst, for Louis-Philippe, this museum, inaugurated in 1837 and devoted to "all of France's glories", reflected a political ambition – to reconcile the partisans of the various successive regimes since 1789 and hence assert his own legitimacy as King of all the French. With more than 6,000 paintings and 3,000 sculptures, it remains the principal iconographic French history source.

◄ Franz Xaver Winterhalter, *Louis-Philippe I, King of the French in the uniform of a general officer*, 1841. Oil on canvas, 284 × 184 cm.

THE HISTORY GALLERIES

THE BATTLE GALLERY

This gallery was created in 1837 by the architects Fontaine and Nepveu. 120 metres long, it occupies most of the South Wing, built in 1681 to house the princes of the royal family. Five beautiful apartments on the first floor and fourteen quarters for courtiers in the attic were destroyed to make way for this gallery commissioned by Louis-Philippe along with the 1830 room next to it.

In thirty-three large paintings and eighty-two busts, the Battle Gallery illustrates the exploits of the major military figures of France. The cycle begins with the depiction of Tolbiac, the founding victory of the French monarchy by Clovis in 496, and ends with that of Napoleon at Wagram in 1809. Other painters involved in fulfilling this prestigious official order were Eugène Delacroix, François Gérard and Horace Vernet.

THE CRUSADES ROOMS

Louis-Philippe created the Crusades Rooms to honour the former families of the nobility who had taken part in these expeditions to the Middle East. Their coats of arms can be seen painted on the ceilings of the five rooms. Originally, he had only planned the biggest of these rooms, which explains why the entire epic story of the eight crusades from the 11th to the 13th century is illustrated there. He had placed there, in the centre of the wall opposite the windows, the large cedar door from the hospital of Saint John of Jerusalem in Rhodes that the Ottoman Sultan had just given him, in 1836. The gothic décor of this door inspired all the decoration of the over-door panels, the chandeliers and the seats which make this suite of rooms one of the most beautiful examples of the "troubadour" style in vogue in the romantic period. It is reported that to meet this order, painters carried out meticulous research using ancient chronicles so that their retrospective works are not only of tremendous artistic quality but also of genuine historic interest.

⬆ Jean-Auguste Bard, *Inauguration of the Battle Gallery, 10 June 1837* (detail), 19th century. Oil on canvas, 66 × 130 cm.

↑ View of the Battle Gallery.

↑ View of the Crusade Room.

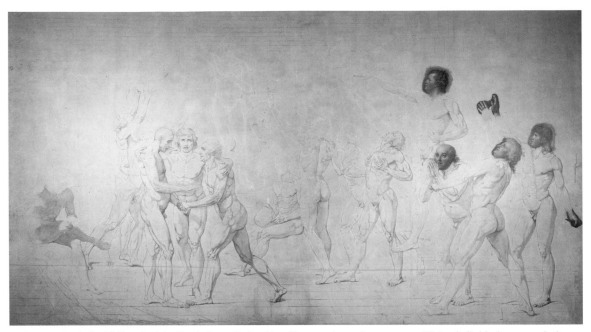

⊕ Jacques-Louis David, Sketch of the *Tennis Court Oath at Versailles on 20 June 1789*, 1791-1792. White chalk, black stone and oil on canvas, 400 × 660 cm.

THE REVOLUTION ROOMS

As one might expect, the Revolution does not enjoy a high profile at Versailles. For this period that was still painful at the time, Louis-Philippe restricted himself to purchasing a few portraits and creating the 1792 room. Located between the Coronation room and the Battle Gallery, this room recalls the victories of the French army as it defended the "country against the dangers it faced", including those at Valmy and Jemmapes; Louis-Philippe had himself portrayed there when he was a young lieutenant general. Today, four other rooms in the Chimay attic, above the Queen's rooms, illustrate the period. In addition to the unfinished canvas of the *Tennis Court Oath at Versailles on 20 June 1789* as well as *Marat assassinated*, outstanding works by the painter David who was a member of the Convention, portraits of Revolution personalities as well as souvenirs of the tragic fate of the royal family are displayed there.

THE 1792 ROOM

The only witness to the days following the Revolution, this room of just under 155 sq.m was redeveloped by Louis-Philippe where the former Merchants Room used to be under the reign of Louis XV, becoming the One Hundred Swiss Room at the time of Louis XVI. It was here that the king assembled the portraits of heroes of the Revolutionary and Empire wars – he is shown as the Duke of Chartres – in their uniforms of 1792 when the Republic was proclaimed. In addition to these various portraits, there are also two compositions after Horace Vernet representing the battles of Valmy and Jemmapes in which the Duke of Chartres and his younger brother the Duke of Montepensier participated. By adorning these historical rooms, Louis-Philippe was no doubt inspired by the continuity of the War Room, the Mirror Room and the Peace Room since the 1792 Room evokes war, the Battle Gallery – by extension – French victories and, further on, the 1830 Room, representing national reconciliation.

THE CORONATION ROOM

This large room was completely transformed in the 19th century when King Louis-Philippe turned Versailles into a museum recounting the history of France up to his own reign through paintings and sculptures. It is therefore attached to the history galleries which today occupy a significant part of the château's wings and other spaces. The paintings there refer to the Napoleonic era, and its name stems from the presence of David's famous composition depicting the crowning ceremony – and not strictly speaking a coronation – of Napoleon I and Josephine, which took place in Notre-Dame de Paris cathedral, on 2 December 1804. It is a replica painted by David himself, between 1808 and 1822 from the first version, today displayed in the Louvre. Under the Ancien Régime, it was the large guardroom which, due to its dimensions and neutral décor, was used for a variety of occasions: for the washing of the feet ceremonies on Maundy Thursday, for "beds of justice" through which the king imposed his will on Parliament and even wedding feasts... Two major compositions, one by David, *The Distribution of Eagles at the Champ-de-Mars* (1804), the other by Gros, *The Battle of Aboukir* (1799), cover the east and north walls. The door lintels painted by Gérard depict *Courage, Genious, Generosity* and *Constance*. The *Allegory of the Eighteen Brumaire* on the ceiling is by Callet.

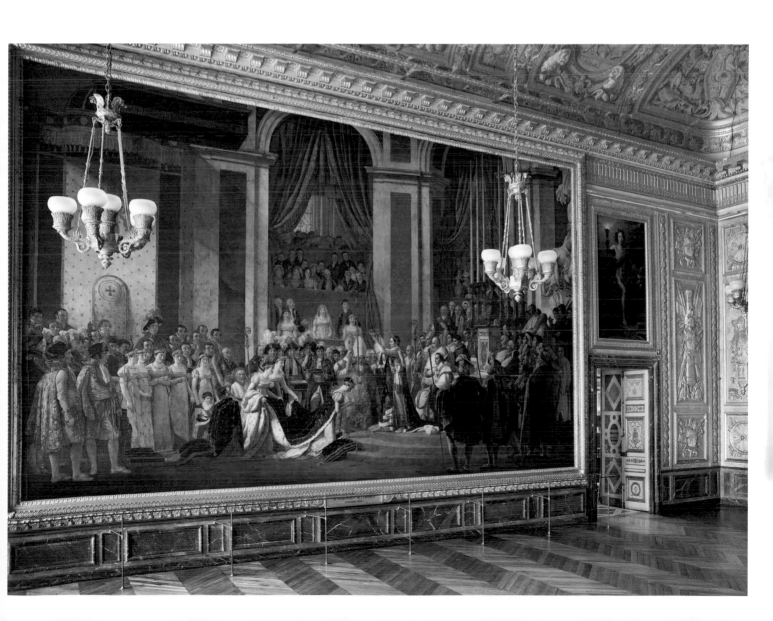

THE CONSULATE AND EMPIRE ROOMS

It is at Versailles that the story of the Napoleonic era is best depicted. It is told in thirty-one rooms distributed between the ground floor of the South Wing and the attics located above. When Louis-Philippe created his museum, there were still numerous and influential partisans of the Emperor, and the subject matter abounds as every artist felt moved to exalt Napoleon's glory. From his accession to power preceding his crowning ceremony on 2 December 1804 until his second abdication in 1815, every aspect of his reign is illustrated: military campaigns in Italy, Egypt and throughout Europe as far as Russia, diplomatic alliances, administrative reorganisation, the imperial family and dignitaries of the regime. As well as being of significant historic interest, the collection stands out for the artistic value of its works, produced by some of the greatest painters of historic events and portraits (Gros, Guérin, Girodet-Trioson, David, Regnault), topographic painters (Lejeune, Bagetti) and sculptors (Houdon, Boizot and Canova).

◐ Antoine-Jean Gros, *General Bonaparte at the Pont d'Arcole, on 17 November 1796*, 1796. Oil on canvas, 130 × 94 cm.
◑ Jacques-Louis David, Bonaparte, *First consul, crossing the Grand Saint-Bernard pass*, 20 May 1800, 19th century. Oil on canvas, 271 × 232 cm.

THE 19TH CENTURY ROOMS

After the 1848 revolution forcing Louis-Philippe into exile, his successors carried on his work. These twenty-one 19th century rooms, located in the attic of the North Wing, illustrate the various periods of the century from the fall of Napoleon I until the Treaty of Versailles: the Restoration (from 1814 to 1830), the July Monarchy (from 1830 to 1848), the Second Empire (from 1852 to 1870), the birth of the Third Republic and the First World War (1914-1918). Military campaigns, scenes of court life, revolutionary days, series of portraits of princes by Gérard and Winterhalter, but also political personalities – such as Thiers, Gambetta and Clémenceau – and artistic personalities – such as Lamartine, Baudelaire, Stendhal, Hugo, Mallarmé, Debussy – extend and complete the history galleries which make up a veritable album of France.

⬆ Jean-Baptiste Guérin Paulin, *Official portrait of Louis XVIII, King of France in grand royal costume*, 1820.
Oil on canvas, 269 × 204 cm.

⬆ Studio of François Pascal Simon Gérard, *Official portrait of Charles X, King of France in grand coronation costume*, 19th century. Oil on canvas, 275 × 202 cm.

➡ Léon Joseph Florentin Bonnat, *Portrait of Victor Hugo*, 1879. Oil on canvas, 138 × 110 cm.

THE COACH GALLERY

The Coach Gallery is located in the Grand Stables built by J. Hardouin-Mansart in 1679-1682. It occupies a gallery that has retained its former appearance, its oak panelling with hay racks and its elegant wrought iron lanterns. The carriages on display were assembled by Louis-Philippe. It was thus that Napoleon Ist's wedding party arrived at Versailles on 2 April 1810 in seven ceremonial coaches evoking the splendour of the imperial court at its height. Also on display is Charles X's coronation carriage, designed by the architect Percier for Louis XVIII, but which the latter never dared use in the political context of the recent Restoration. Louis-Philippe also purchased sedan-chairs and sleighs; the latter were already at Versailles under the Ancien Régime when they were used for racing along the snow-covered paths of the grounds or on the frozen Grand Canal. In 1833, Louis XVIII's funeral carriage joined these vehicles; it is the only remaining example of a royal funeral hearse.

⊕ Jean-Baptiste Martin, the Elder, *The Stables with a view of the Château de Versailles*, 18th century. Oil on canvas, 260 × 184 cm.

⊕ Charles X's coronation carriage built in 1821.

⊕ View of the Coach Gallery from the Château de Versailles..

CHRONOLOGY

VERSAILLES

1623-1624 Louis XIII has a hunting lodge built at Versailles.

1631 Louis XIII asks Philibert Le Roy to build a château on the site of the hunting lodge.

1643 Louis XIII stays at Versailles for the last time.

1660 Marriage of Louis XIV to Maria Theresa of Austria. The King brings his wife to Versailles on October 25.

1664 Festivities of the Pleasures of the Enchanted Isle.

1668 Great royal entertainment at Versailles.

1668-1670 Construction of outer shell of Le Vau.

1677-1689 Large-scale building work at Versailles under the guidance of Hardouin-Mansart (the Ministers' Wing, the Stables and the South Wing, the Grand Lodgings and the North Wing)

1682 Louis XIV designates Versailles as the official residence of the Court and seat of government.

1684 Completion of the construction of the Hall of Mirrors.

1710 Consecration of the Chapel Royal on June 5.

1715 1 September, death of Louis XIV. 9 September, Louis XV abandons Versailles for Vincennes.

1722 Louis XV returns to live at Versailles.

1736 26 September, opening of the Hercules Salon.

1757 Attempt on Louis XV's life by Damiens.

1768 The Petit Trianon is completed.

1770 Official opening of the Opera Royal by Gabriel.

1774 May 10, Louis XV dies of smallpox at Versailles.

1777 Visit of Joseph II, Emperor of Austria, the Queen's brother.

1783 Signing of the Treaty of Versailles, acknowledging the independence of the United States of America.

1783-1786 Construction of the Queen's Hamlet.

1789 5 May, opening of the States General; 20 June, "Tennis Court Oath"; 6 October, the King, the Royal Family and the Court leave Versailles for good.

1837 10 June, Louis-Philippe inaugurates the museum dedicated to the glories of France.

IN FRANCE

1624 Start of the ministry of Richelieu.

1631 Théophraste Renaudot founds the first weekly newspaper: *La Gazette*.

1638 Birth of Louis XIV in Saint-Germain-en-Laye.

1643 14 May, death of Louis XIII.

1661 Death of Mazarin, start of personal reign by Louis XIV. Colbert is appointed superintendent of finance.

1668 Jean de La Fontaine begins publishing his *Fables*.

1682 The assembly of the clergy adopts the Declaration of the four articles, the charter of political and religious Gallicanism.

1684 Ratisbonne truce between France and the German Empire.

1685 Revocation of the Edict of Nantes.

1710 Destruction of the Abbey of Port-Royal des Champs.

1714 End of the war of the Spanish succession.

1722 Marivaux publishes *La Surprise de l'amour*.

1757 Signature of a new Treaty of Versailles; Russia, Saxony and Sweden join the Franco-Austrian alliance.

1768 15 May, France purchases Corsica from the Republic of Genoa.

1777 Publication of the first daily newspaper: *La Gazette de Paris*.

1783 First balloon flights by the Montgolfier brothers (4 June at Annonay, 19 September at Versailles.)

1787 6 August, Louis XVI calls a "bed of justice"

1789 14 July, storming of the Bastille.

1837 30 May, France signs the Treaty of Tafna with Abd-el-Kader in Algeria. 30 October, the French capture Constantinople.

BIOGRAPHIES
KINGS AND QUEENS AT VERSAILLES

LOUIS XIII (1601-1643)

It was at Versailles, that the six-year-old Dauphin discovered hunting for the first time. Much taken with the location, he gave orders for the first château to be built there in 1623-1624. However, the construction was soon the subject of ridicule and he therefore had it demolished to make way for a new hunting lodge in 1631-1634. It was in this residence reserved for private use and his companions in arms that he decided to support Richelieu during the Day of the Dupes on 10 November 1630. This somewhat timid and melancholic king also used Versailles as a refuge, most notably when Mademoiselle de La Fayette retired to the convent in 1637. The château remained unchanged until the king's death in 1643.

The studio of Justus Van Egmont,
Louis XIII in cuirassed bust (detail),
17th century. Oil on canvas, 76.5 × 65 cm.

LOUIS XIV (1638-1715)

Like his father before him, Louis XIV discovered Versailles thanks to hunting. Ill at ease in the largely urbanised capital, the king viewed Versailles as an opportunity to satisfy his appetite for construction. He took the view that glory was founded on both conquests and buildings. Despite its somewhat patchwork appearance, Versailles thus became his masterpiece. More than an edifice, Louis XIV used it to build a concept: the installation not only of his court but also of his government. The perfect embodiment of power, he died on 1 September 1715 in the master bedroom at the centre of the château after declaring: "I may be departing but the State shall remain forever."

After Hyacinthe Rigaud, *Louis XIV,
King of France* (detail), 17th-18th centuries.
Oil on canvas, 81 × 65 cm.

MARIA THERESA OF AUSTRIA (1638-1683)

Contrary to Anne of Austria who never stayed overnight at Versailles, Maria-Theresa resided in the château for a period of four months after her marriage with Louis XIV in October 1660. Her suite was in the South Wing, symmetrical to that of the king. Somewhat unassuming in nature, the queen, who left little to remember her by, had to suffer the effrontery of the numerous mistresses which her husband installed in Versailles, sometimes in apartments bigger than her own. She died in the space of five days from a seemingly benign tumour on 30 July 1683.

Jean Nocret, *Maria-Theresa of Austria,
Infanta of Spain, Queen of France* (detail),
17th century. Oil on canvas, 150.5 × 178 cm.

LOUIS XV (1710-1774)

François-Hubert Drouais, Louis XV,
King of France and Navarre (detail),
August 1773. Oil on canvas, 73 × 59 cm.

With almost no surviving family, Louis XV was the first king to be born at Versailles. Melancholic or even morbid in temperament, the sovereign was ill-suited to the straightjacket of customs imposed by his great-grandfather, Louis XIV. Despite adjustments to ensure greater privacy, he endeavoured to retain the main principles of etiquette and terminated the work initiated under the previous reign – the Neptune Basin and construction of the Opera – while regularly fleeing to other residences such as Choisy, Bellevue and La Muette. In 1774, the people of Versailles celebrated the demise of the king initially dubbed Louis Le Bien Aimé (Louis the well-beloved) but who turned out to be a libertine.

MARIE LESZCZYNSKA (1703-1768)

Studio of Jean-Marc Nattier, *Marie Leszczynska,
Queen of France* (detail), 18th century.
Oil on canvas, 146.5 × 113.7 cm.

Daughter of the deposed king of Poland, Stanislas Leszczynski, Marie was to have an extraordinary destiny: marriage in 1725 to the most powerful king in Europe, seven years her junior. Propelled to Versailles, the queen rapidly refused all cliques and proved above board in every respect. A great music lover, she introduced concerts to the Salon of Peace. A loyal wife, she gave Louis XV no fewer than eight daughters and two sons in the space of ten years. A feat which inspired the lyrics "forever reclining, forever fat, forever in labour". Bearing her husband's peccadilloes with a certain dignity, she was always treated with considerable respect.

LOUIS XVI (1754-1793)

Joseph Siffred Duplessis, Louis XVI,
King of France and Navarre (detail),
1778. Oil on canvas, 80 × 62 cm.

Born in Versailles, Louis XVI was the last king to live there. Along with a palace, he also inherited a burdensome tradition which his grandfather Louis XV had already begun to abandon. Apart from minor redevelopments for greater comfort, he kept the château as it was when he took possession in 1774. To meet expectations, he undertook reforms of the royal household leading to the reduction of his domestic staff which also contributed to the deconsecration of his person. On 5 and 6 October 1789, he was brought back to Paris with his family and forced to accept the constitutional monarchy. With the French Revolution in full cry, he was arrested, put on trial and found guilty. Louis XVI was guillotined on 21 January 1793.

Studio of Élisabeth Louise Vigée-Le Brun,
Marie Antoinette, Queen of France (detail),
18th century. Oil on canvas, 65 × 55 cm.

MARIE-ANTOINETTE (1755-1793)

It was at the tender age of 15, that Marie-Antoinette arrived at Versailles from Vienna. Bearing the title of dauphine to the most glamorous court in Europe and fascinated by luxury and entertainment, she struck a marked contrast with her husband who was more inclined towards the simple things in life. Despite a strict, Habsburgian upbringing, she failed to fully master the codes of French etiquette which - contrary to that of Vienna - drew no distinction between public and private life. Initially acclaimed, the young queen, who had a penchant for music and fashion, soon became a source of irritation because of her indiscretions. Caught up in the horrors of the French Revolution, she suffered the same fate as her husband and was guillotined on 16 October 1793.

BIOGRAPHIES
VERSAILLES CRAFTSMEN

Jean-Baptiste Mauzaisse, after Nicolas de Largillière,
Portrait of Charles Le Brun, painter (detail),
19th century. Oil on canvas, diameter: 95 cm.

CHARLES LE BRUN (1619-1690)

Apprentice to François Perrier and enjoying the protection of the Chancellor Séguier who recommended him to Simon Vouet, Le Brun began working as a society painter. In 1642, he accompanied Poussin to Rome where he spent three years copying Raphael and works from classical antiquity. Soon spotted for his talent, he was tasked by Foucquet with decorating Vaux, without restricting himself to painting. Louis XIV took him under his wing in 1661, making him his principal painter in 1664 and then entrusting him the same year with the "supervision and general custody of the cabinet of paintings and drawings of His Majesty". From the early 1660s onwards, he would be the main commissioner of the interior decorations at Versailles.

Carlo Maratta, *André Le Nôtre (1613-1700),*
controller of buildings and designer of the king's gardens
(detail), 1679. Oil on canvas, 112 × 85 cm.

ANDRÉ LE NÔTRE (1613-1700)

Born into a family of gardeners connected to all the leading specialists of the era, Le Nôtre learnt his trade at Tuileries then at the Châuteau de Vaux-le-Vicomte working for Foucquet. This was where he earned his reputation as general supervisor of the king's buildings and gardens. At Versailles, he was the authorising officer for all the gardens, allowing him to give full rein to his artistic bent by drawing up the plans for groves, avenues and perspectives in accordance with the sun's daytime trajectory while playing on east-west and north-south axes. Up until his death, the gardener had not only earned the trust of Louis XIV but with it his friendship.

LOUIS LE VAU (1612-1670)

After being trained by the Villedo construction firm on projects in Paris, Le Vau worked on urbanisation of the capital's Ile Saint-Louis with the construction of seventeen houses and private mansions - including those of Lambert and Lauzun. He became the chief architect of the king in 1654. At the same time, at the head of his agency, he took responsibility for constructing the Château de Vaux for Foucquet. After the superintendent's fall from grace, Louis XIV tasked Le Vau with upgrading and extending Versailles. So it was that he came to design an outer shell for these three Baroque style buildings which are embedded in the old château of Louis XIII to the south, west and north opening onto the gardens.

Claude Lefebvre, *Jean-Baptiste Colbert,*
minister (detail), 1666.
Oil on canvas, 130 × 96 cm.

JEAN-BAPTISTE COLBERT (1619-1683)

Colbert rose through the ranks of the royal administration to attain the prestigious post of Controller-General of Finances in 1661 as well as Superintendent of Buildings. He was therefore directly concerned by the construction of Versailles in two respects. Although he never fully understood Louis XIV's strong attachment to this residence, alerting the king to the sizeable financial outlays on several occasions, the minister proved to be a skilful servant who did his utmost to ensure the project's success.

JULES HARDOUIN-MANSART (1646-1708)

Great nephew of François Mansart on his mother's side, Jules Hardouin cleverly pinned the famous surname to his own on his great uncle's death in 1666 having worked with him on Parisian projects. He won his spurs at Clagny in 1675 with the château of Madame de Montespan, a favourite of Louis XIV, then the following year worked on projects at Versailles over which he had full control. The chief architect in practice, he was formally appointed to this post in 1681 before also taking on the prestigious role of general supervisor of buildings in 1699.

François de Troy, *Jules Hardouin-Mansart, architect, superintendent of buildings* (detail), 18th century. Oil on canvas, 132 × 98 cm.

ANGE JACQUES GABRIEL (1698-1782)

Part of a long dynasty of builders and architects active since the 17th century, Gabriel soon joined the service of the king's buildings to work at Versailles. He became principal architect to the king in 1742 on the death of his father Jacques V, assuming responsibility for all projects at Versailles. In particular, he was responsible for the Petit Trianon and the Opera Royal, as well as the most stunning interiors of Louis XV's suite. The king's death in 1774 halted his career in its tracks; although he just had time to complete the library of Louis XVI the following year.

Jean-Baptiste Greuze, French school, *Jacques Gabriel, architect* (detail), 18th century. Oil on canvas, 65 × 54 cm.

RICHARD MIQUE (1728-1794)

Son and grandson of architects from Nancy, Mique began working under the orders of Stanislas Leszczynski in Lorraine where he developed the antique neo-classical style of the Renaissance at the Château de Nancy and the Château de Lunéville. This allowed him to establish a reputation and, in 1766, the queen called him to Versailles to build a convent for her – now the Hoche high school. Shunned by Gabriel who was wary of his influence, he regained prominence thanks to Marie-Antoinette who as a firm supporter allowed him to become principal architect to the king in 1775. Accused of conspiring to save the queen, he was sentenced to death on 7 July 1794 and guillotined the following day at the Place du Trône-Renversé – now Place de la Nation.

Jean-Ernest Heinsius, *Richard Mique, architect* (detail), 1782. Oil on canvas, 65 × 54.5 cm. Nancy, Lorraine Museum.

**Établissement public du château,
du musée et du domaine national de Versailles**

Jean-Vincent Bacquart,
head of the publishing department,
assisted by *Corinne Thépaut-Cabasset*
head of publishing

Réunion des musées nationaux–Grand Palais

Director of publishing
Sophie Laporte

Head of publications
Muriel Rausch

Editorial coordination
Lucile Desmoulins

PAO
Hervé Delemotte

Production
Hugues Charreyron

Graphic design
Établissement P&J

Translation
Ilti

Maps
Thierry Lebreton and Dominique Bissière
Jean-François Péneau

Photo-engraving
Axiome

Printing
Graphius

Page 2: The 'Royal' gates at night.
Page 3: The fountains of the Neptune Basin in operation, in the grounds of the Château of Versailles.
Page 4: Elisabeth Louise Vigée-LeBrun, Portrait of Queen Marie-Antoinette 'à la rose' (holding a rose), 1783.
Oil on canvas. 113 x 87 cm.
Page 5: The Petit Trianon, le salon de compagnie (public salon).
Page 6: Jean Warin, Louis XIV, 1671-1672. Marble statue, 208 x 104 x 62 cm.

Unless otherwise stated, all of the works reproduced are housed at the national museum of the Châteaux of Versailles and Trianon.